A **Year A** Resource

Contemporary
Reflections
for praying & preaching

Sheila Walker

kevin
mayhew

First published in 2007 by

KEVIN MAYHEW LTD
Buxhall, Stowmarket, Suffolk, IP14 3BW
info@kevinmayhewltd.com
www.kevinmayhew.com

9 8 7 6 5 4 3 2 1 0

ISBN 978 184417 824 7
Catalogue No. 1501038

Cover design by Sara-Jane Came
Edited by Sophia Sorrell
Typesetting by Richard Weaver

Printed and bound in Great Britain

Contents

EASTER

ORDINARY TIME

Foreword

I remember one edition of *Desert Island Discs* when the castaway, informed that he could take the Bible and Shakespeare with him, told the interviewer: 'You can keep the Bible!'. I can't remember what he took instead; I can only hope that one day he'll come to regret that decision.

In our country today we are fast losing that almost instinctive respect for the Bible, along with the collective folk memory of some of its gems. Different versions abound, but its readership has not multiplied accordingly. Yet in the Bible, uniquely, are the words of eternal life, words which on every encounter seem to create, to reveal, to touch, to illumine something fresh: surprising, delighting and challenging, coloured scarves and live rabbits from the magician's hat, truth which sets us free.

These reflections make no great claims to be either scholarly or thorough, balanced or religious: they are personal, as are all reflections, and I am none of those things. It is simply how the Common Worship readings from the Bible resonated with me, triggered questions, comforted or discomforted me: my prayer is that, as you read, God will surprise, delight and challenge you, too, in a way that would make the Bible your castaway's first choice, every time.

SHEILA WALKER

Advent

98, 99, 100 – Coming!

Isaiah 2:1-5; Matthew 24:36-44

What if . . .
all our Christmas cards
were about the *second* coming?
I guess we might think twice
before sending them to most of our friends;
hardly cosy,
hardly what we're used to at this time of year . . .

'The baby's on the way,
coming very soon –
bound to be in the next few weeks;
meanwhile, busy ourselves
with all those tiny garments,
shake out granny's christening robe . . .'

No.

The King is on the way,
coming – how soon?
Bound to be when we least expect it;
meanwhile, what of our garments, our dirty linen?
Whether we wash it in public or in private
it won't come clean;
only the robe of the righteousness of Christ
will protect us from the gaze of the all-seeing one.

Christmas is coming
with all its fairy lights,
its twinkly technology,
its 'atmosphere' . . .
And we look back, we prefer to look back
to the certainties of the past:

that a baby was born, and lived, and died
and although he was special,
taught like an angel,
and it was a shame about his extremely unpleasant death,
some would say, 'Well, nothing much has really changed – has it?
For the most part, history carries on regardless;
men still beat their ploughshares into swords
their pruning hooks into spears.
Nation still takes up machete, Kalashnikov or guided missile against nation
and child soldiers inherit a taste and a talent for war,
the sins of the fathers to the third and fourth generation.

'And there's little sign
of Jerusalem, the mountain of God,
being the promised haven of peace and justice,
a beacon to the nations,
a sanctuary for those who love the Lord.
Far from it.
Yet if all the world's a stage
Jerusalem is set to be the scene
for the final act in this earthly drama.'

And that time will come . . .

And here in Advent
we are not about looking backwards to Christmas
but forwards.
Next time
we will not be charmed by the fairy lights
but electrified by the Light of the World,
the Light that will do away with the need for sun and moon.
Next time
no star over a stable, whatever its wonder and royal beauty
but the bright Morning Star
Christ clothed in a blaze of glory,
the King coming to take his power and reign:
and all shall see
and all shall know
and every knee shall bow.

No. Not cosy.

It's one thing to pray
'Thy Kingdom come'
and quite another to welcome the King
who comes to divide and rule
to send his angels to sort out the wheat from the tares
to divide the sheep from the goats
to take one and leave another.

What a day that will be!
When the magician's assistant vanishes for real . . .
When the premiership becomes 5 a side . . .
When the preacher prays for an empty church . . .

We can see the funny side now
but then –
how we will long to be taken,
to be among those who have made Christ King,
those good and faithful servants
who have taken their cross and followed him,
who have traded their rags
for his robe of righteousness.

But what of the rest?
My son, my friend, my colleague,
the sceptic, the busy, the bored –
What of them?

We can only tell, tell them the whole story;
not just baby talk
but the epic tale of the one who was, and who is
and who is to come . . .

For that day is coming –
and is nearer now than when we first believed –
that day that Advent holds in view
when God declares again –
and this time the whole world hears –

that history is his story
and all things find their meaning, and their resolution
only in him.
God will be seen to be God,
dictators will be humbled,
experts confounded,
the proud most reluctantly abandoned,
the rich sent empty away . . .

. . . 98 . . . 99 . . . 100 . . . I'm coming!

Where will he find me?
When the Son of Man comes, will he find faith on the earth?

Let us walk in the light of the Lord.

Where will he find me?
No hiding in shadowy corners
for the darkness is as light to him and there can be
no hiding from the all-seeing one.

Let us walk in the light of the Lord

for then he is our friend and brother
and his blood makes us clean, and he will find us
ready
always ready
for his coming.

Living in Hope

Isaiah 11:1-10; Psalm 72:1-7; 18, 19

Hope is a strange land to live in;
for some, little more than a misty marshland
of wishful thinking;
for others, firm ground beneath the feet
and already the hint of gold on the horizon
heralding sunrise.

Israel,
finding it too hard
to hold on to their hope in an invisible God
found instead Saul;
why, you had only to look at him!
Head and shoulders above the rest of them,
surely Saul would deliver them from the fear of their enemies,
surely Saul would be the king above all kings?
They lived in hope.

And when Saul failed them
as people are apt to do
(especially those we put on pedestals)
well, there was David,
the golden boy, the man after God's own heart: surely he . . . ?
And then Solomon,
munificent architect of that magnificent temple,
renowned for his wisdom and wealth: surely he . . . ?
They lived in hope.

But no.
The kingliness of the invisible God
proved too hot for mere mortals to handle
and, one after the other,
crowned heads were turned

by power, spun and crumbled into ruin
as the rot set in and the royal family tree
was finally felled:
hope grounded.

Until,
from the tree stump
a pale, brave, incongruous shoot
broke, almost unnoticed,
through the dark mouldy stuff.
What would become of it?

And we, we hopefuls, are we the same?
Finding it too hard
to hold on to any hope we may ever have had in an invisible God,
do we count on a change of prime minister,
party or president –
or have we lost even that meagre hope,
reckoning 'politicians are all the same . . .'?

And do we then lower our sights,
hope for less:
that the children will pass their exams and find work;
that Dad's cancer will go into remission,
that it'll stay fine for the big match
and I'll find a nice coat in the charity shop:
is that too much to hope for,
God – is that too much to ask?

No. It is too little.
And yet – yes, maybe it is too much.

Come on, I want you to dig deep into your soul,
tell me what you *really* hope,
you know, 'If you could have three wishes . . .'
(True, I am not your fairy godmother
 but I am, in fact, God.)
Tell me about your longing for peace,
for a world where those who have plenty
are prodigal, the poor belong to the past

and the future is free.
Tell me: I'm listening, and your cry
echoes in my heart
echoes my heart.

And your lesser hopes,
nudged to the surface by the day's needs,
I hear them too;
they are part of that great cacophony,
my world sounding off,
from which I must distil a symphony.

The tree was felled:
but what of that maverick shoot?

First choice of route I cannot guarantee,
but safe arrival at your hoped-for destination,
yes: for the shoot is the first planting
and the first seeding
of the new Eden:
anchor your hope in nothing less
than its good earth
and the certainty of its springing eternal.

For the peace, the perfection for which you hope
is there, though it lies on the other side
of judgement, and redemption:
will you walk through these?
For there are no easy answers,
no quick healing of my people's wounds,
no saying 'Peace!' where there is no justice,
no saying 'Hope!' where there is no willingness
to walk the way of the cross . . .

To be free from persecution, prejudice must welcome light;
    greed must learn grace;
to be free from poverty, wealth must be cast on the water;
    fat cat and church mouse embrace;
to be free from abuse, anger must yield without a fight
    and face down,

as our trees are felled
and the whole earth is judged by that maverick shoot,
God's perfect King

not equipped with the Spirit of God for an uncertain term
but that very Spirit personified;
until that day when the glory of God
puts the sun and the moon out of business
and we live not in hope
but *there*, in the hoped-for,
sufficient presence of God himself.

Magnifi-chat

Luke 1:46-55

Well, you can understand Mary being a bit high,
can't you, on cloud nine or so
after the angel happened by.
But I do sometimes wonder – I hope not too irreverently –
what planet she was on
when she sang that song
that we have taken on and done to death: Magnificat.

My soul glorifies the Lord,
my spirit rejoices in God my Saviour
I mean, it's all very well for you, lass,
singled out for special treatment,
basking in the golden glow of being chosen . . .
For he has been mindful
of the humble state of his servant
Yes, one in a million –
about as much chance as becoming Miss Universe,
and you landed it!
But what about the other teenage mums
whose humble state seems to have passed him by,
who are still queuing for rice in the refugee camp,
still watching helplessly as their child dies of Aids
or, like my friend Jas in a very humble estate south of the river,
still waiting for a council flat
that doesn't need protecting by an oversized underfed guard dog?

All generations will call me blessed,
for the Mighty One has done great things for me
Will we call you 'blessed'?
In one sense, yes – unutterably, to be chosen
for such an inconceivable task,

making God in our image, no less:
but chosen, too, for fear, for flight
for frustration, misunderstanding,
ridicule and heartbreak –
which has led us muddled thinkers to latch on
not to the privilege of being chosen
but to your understanding, participation in grief and loss;
so to latch on to you as go-between
(what happened to the one mediator between God and man??)
and even worship you alongside God . . .
Did you realise it would come to this?
Aren't you horrified, dismayed?

His mercy is on those who fear him,
from generation to generation'
But what of the generations who have lost that fear:
what grandparents revered
their children relegated,
grandchildren rubbished;
– what mercy then?

He has performed mighty deeds,
scattered those who are proud in their inmost thoughts;
he has brought down rulers from their thrones
but has lifted up the humble
Mighty deeds, yes – and many, maybe, assigned
to another, or to chance, being unsigned;
but as we confess also our sins of omission,
what of the Almighty's undone deeds?
Don't you watch the news, Lord, see the film footage
deemed too shocking to show?
Why? Why so many, so few, so long, so slow?
The proud still seem pretty comfortably ensconced
in well-known addresses:
for every proud despot deposed
a prouder one who brings about his downfall;
for every power-hungry ruler hounded out
a hungrier one stands waiting in the wings.

Humility and power seldom walk together:
still the humble wait in hundreds and thousands
for that lift.

He has filled the hungry with good things
but has sent the rich away empty
Oh, it's all very well to *spiritualise* these things,
but even those who hunger for God
go hungry where scripture is banned
or still in a foreign tongue;
young disciples so often denied freedom,
work, education, a reasonable living
while the rich still have the key to the door
they have locked from the inside.
And the physically hungry are counted in millions
by the rich who have time, and ease,
and nothing better to do than sit and count . . .
And as for being filled with *good* things –
when the golden arches are more widely recognised
than the cross
and half the Western world is obese,
while the rest pick weevils from the wheat
and suck chicken's feet –
Well, Lord,
I don't think you'd get many stars
in the Michelin guide
(though maybe sending Jamie Oliver
was a start).

He has helped his servant Israel
remembering to be merciful
to Abraham and his descendants for ever
Well, OK: looking back at the Old Testament
there were some pretty sticky patches:
rebellion, wilderness, exile,
but I guess you could say, in his anger
God remembered mercy
and the survival of the Jews, against all odds,

must count as good evidence
for the existence of their God.
But what of the wars, the famines, the misrule
that went so long unchecked, Mary?
To say nothing of your people's later history:
scattergun, scorched earth, holocaust,
which hardly suggests favour . . .

So, Mary, where were you coming from?
Did God in you speak, seeing with his eyes,
seeing what one day will be
as though it has already happened,
is already true?

The burden of waiting to be delivered
from evil
can weigh heavy;
I, too,
could use such a view.

A Night to Remember

Isaiah 7:10-16; Psalm 80:1-7, 17-19; Romans 1:1-7; Matthew 1:18-25

He was so looking forward to it.

Not easy to be patient for so long, when the sight of her set your blood
    racing,
when at night you had to school your thoughts:
but the year was almost ended,
the pledge soon to be redeemed –
soon, now, they would be together, be one.

He and Mary
Mary, so young, yet so – composed, so assured, so *true*:
or so he thought.

Which was why it hit him so hard,
the news that she had given him with apprehension, yes: but with an
    excitement,
an awe which belied the fact that it couldn't possibly be true.
The father, that is: there was, it seemed, no doubt about the pregnancy.

How could he have been so wrong about her?
Others, yes: more, perhaps, than you might guess
defaulted on the agreement. But Mary? He was so sure
she was special.
And to have come up with such a ludicrous, extravagant story seemed –
almost blasphemous.
And from one with such a quiet piety. So much for appearances.
What, who could you trust now?
Yes, to be sure there would be others – eventually. But who's to say
that any could be trusted, now?

But all that would come later. For the moment, there was Mary.
For all she would shame him, he would not shame her,

nor harm her; divorce her, yes: quickly, quietly
and let time bring its accommodation.

It would do no good to delay; not for her, nor for him.
What must be done, must be done now, he told himself:
listen to your head, Joseph, not to the longing
nor the creeping, bitter disillusion of your heart . . .

'I'll sleep on it,' he thought: 'this one last night; tomorrow,
then, will see it done: and God have mercy on us both,
she bearing the fruit of betrayal, inviting rejection:
I its willing and unwilling agent.'

And so he slept, fitfully, tossing
between feverish indignation and cold despair;
hoping against hope he could wake
and find it was all a dream.

So soon, it seemed, it was morning:
but no! This light was too bright, brighter than any dawn
and too soon for dawn, and so bright he could see through closed eyes
that he was not alone

and he lay still, quite, quite still
in case the least movement should offend or disturb
the visitor: though he had never entertained such a stranger, nor even
the thought, he knew the angel

and stilled his mind, waiting,
waiting between utmost joy and deepest trepidation
for the bright messenger to deliver him
words for good or ill, which he could only agree . . .
and all the time the light blazed, so many lasers etching on his mind
the night he would always remember.

And the words, which seemed to ring
from the beginning of time, down through the ages,
finding their echo in the mouth of the prophets, and now in his own ears,
describing his own destiny:

'Joseph, son of David,
remember who you are! You, too, have a place in history.
do not be afraid to take Mary,
not afraid of name-calling, of gossip, of priding myself on my magnanimity
because what is conceived in her is from the Holy Spirit.
What!? You mean it's true?
O, my God.
Joseph, are you listening? There's more . . .!
What? More?
You are to call the child Jesus, because he will save his people from their sins.'
Jesus. God saves.
O God, forgive me. Mary, forgive me.
Mary! You and me . . . together . . .

And he woke to find that indeed it had all been a dream,
Mary's deceit a delusion, his worst fears a mere nightmare,
the blasphemy his, not hers;
but the angel! The angel was no mere dream, but a glimpse
into a world more real than the one he now contemplated with new eyes,
pondering the day's purpose
in the light of the night
he would always remember:

and would need to remember
each time he saw the pity in their glance,
heard the whispers, wiped the tears that sprung, unbidden
in spite of Mary's resolution;
and when the child grew and behaved strangely,
to their way of thinking, disturbed them with his learning
and left them, then, often: and they would hear only rumours
of his wonders, and his wisdom
and his rabble rousing, and his ruthless dissection of the religious right.
Rumours, too, of how it would all end in tears.

And did he live to see the end?
Remembering still that night
to set against the despair and horror of those final hours
when every promise seemed empty, every hope betrayed,
every vision only make-believe?

There, in the utter darkness
held still by that bright angel he could not deny,
that night more real than any day before or since
etched on his soul?
Held until the sun rose on the third day,
and his son rose on that third day
and his angel, and every angel in the entire universe
sang, and sang
and danced with Joseph
and in their eyes the merest hint,
'Told you so!'

Christmas

Title Deeds

Isaiah 9:2-7

Wonderful Counsellor

Wonderful, for a start, that words spoken by Isaiah
seven hundred years before
should travel safely through so many ages, and arrive
expectant, at *that* stable door,

recognising in that backroom baby
the child with an insatiable thirst
for wisdom; who would linger in the temple, putting
his heavenly Father's business first,

recognising in that eager child
the carpenter whose hammer blows
would bring the old religion crashing down,
the sacrificial system to a close

saying – 'And now for something completely different!'
and the wise men, those who had eyes
to see, laid down their swords and pens,
recognised in him the wisest of the wise.

Received wisdom, though,
is rarely flavour of the month today;
old wineskins can't contain heady new wine
which says 'No thanks: I'll do it *my* way!'

Strange, then, that we have so many counsellors,
think-tanks and therapists, quality controls,
consultancies, advisers, mentoring
life coaches and opinion polls . . .

Do we secretly still doubt ourselves?
How *am* I doing? Have I got it right?
What *is* it all about? Who do I ask, whose
answer can I trust? Where is the *true* light?

Truly, there is only one most Wonderful Counsellor:
Jesus Christ, son and heir to all the wisdom of God.

Mighty God

The fact that the world keeps turning
with seeming indifference in the face of so much grief
has made it hard for us to think of God as mighty:
surely his power *or* his love must be beyond belief?

Why doesn't God just *do* something
to make this world a happier, more peaceful place?
I wonder what, exactly, we'd suggest –
short of simply airbrushing the human race.

Even those who don't buy into God
look at the power lines and wonder whether,
among those multi-nationals, media moguls, Mafiosi,
might and right will ever come together?

And would we ever in a million years
have guessed at a divine solution
that countered human power with – meekness?
Astonishing, subversive revolution:

Jesus – meek, but mighty in word, proclaiming the truth of God;
Jesus – meek, but mighty in thought, discerning the wisdom of God;
Jesus – meek, but mighty in deed, serving the purpose of God;
Jesus – meek, but mighty in love, expressing the heart of God;

mighty because he was free from fear and pride,
mighty because he was free from the need to be driven,
mighty because in the end he had nothing to lose
except for his life: and that he had already given.

The might of our mighty God
is not military might, or media might, or monetary might;
not force of character, force of will or force of circumstance;
it is not force at all.
The true might of our mighty God
is life-giving
sacrificial
love.

Truly, there is only one Mighty God:
Jesus, our Saviour by the power of the cross.

Everlasting Father

It should be such a wonderful thought,
the fatherhood of God; but we have moved so far;
with paternity disputes and all mum's boyfriends,
so many of us wonder who our fathers *are*

or even if we want to know, if he's the one
who left us in the lurch, chased by the CSA,
who turns up, looking wretched and distraught
to take us out, while mother looks the other way . . .

What's in our mind, then, as we come to pray
'Our Father'? How can we reclaim
the guiding hand, example, warmth, security,
that should be part and parcel of that name?

Jesus said: 'He who has seen me has seen the Father.'
'Let the children come to me.'
'I will never, ever leave you.'
'I am the truth, and I will set you free.'

If you never knew that safe place behind a father's coat,
that awe at his wisdom and skill,
that excitement when he said 'Come on, let's go!'
being carried up a hill;
if you never knew that love, and awe at his voice,

that strong arm around you
that look of sheer delight that his child
was lost, but he found you –

it's never too late
our Father God has signed the adoption papers
and is waiting to bring us home.

Truly, there is only one Everlasting Father
who, in Jesus, invites us into his kingdom as the children we are . . .

Prince of Peace

Whatever did he mean – saying
'I come *not* to bring peace but a sword'
Yet at the same time 'Peace I leave with you,
a peace not of this world . . . '?

Ah, there perhaps is the clue:
not as the world gives, Jesus said . . .
So when the angels sang of peace on earth
as the baby slept in his makeshift bed

they sang, it says, of goodwill *to* men
not goodwill *between* men. Ah,
goodwill, then, from God to men: no way
a promise of an end to war.

For outward conflict cannot cease
until the conflicts of the heart and mind,
the insecurity, the greed, the lust for power
cease to be the curse of all mankind.

And this, even this, is the great gift of Christmas:
Gold – the promise of peace in my soul
    setting me free to love
Frankincense – the promise of peace in my spirit
    setting me free to worship
Myrrh – the promise of peace in my heart
    setting me free even to suffer with joy.

Truly, the peace of God,
passing all human understanding,
keeps our hearts and minds
as they hush their demanding,
consent to be still
and accept from his hand
that in spite of apparent ill,
all is for good in all he has planned.

In this world, we will have trouble: that is a promise;
but in our hearts, we can have peace: that is a greater promise.

Truly, there is only one Prince of Peace:
Jesus, who gives us, this Christmas, his hard-won peace to rule in our hearts.

I Know How You Feel

Isaiah 63:7-9; Hebrews 2:10-18

When he died, my friend said
'I'm not going to say "I know how you feel"
because I don't
and I don't want to know, because I couldn't bear it.'

And it's true. None of us really knows –
or perhaps wants to know – how someone else feels,
the peculiar complexities of *that* grief, *that* pain;
we tell ourselves we need to keep a little distance,
resist being dragged into their darkness
if we're to remain firm friends,
able to offer any light, any relief: and perhaps it's true.

But for the one who suffers –
nothing, then, to mitigate that awful isolation,
that sense that no one else can fully understand;
that everything offered, however well-meaning, is of necessity
partial, superficial, provisional
because the breadth and the depth of my suffering
are mine alone.

But then I read
'In *all* their distress, God too was distressed,'
and I am incredulous!
To think that God suffered
persecution, temptation of every kind,
ridicule, misunderstanding, violence, betrayal
and all the anguish of crucifixion . . .

Yet it was one life, you say, and there came a point
when his suffering came to an end
while the world suffers still.

But somehow, from day one till kingdom come
the suffering of this fallen world cries out across time
and the one on the cross, in a moment of time, receives
the unique, unimaginable pain of the world's sin:

in *all* our distress
God was then, and is, and will be
distressed. Though beyond his world,
binding himself so closely to it,
investing himself so completely in it
he feels our every wound
and by his wounds we feel, and are healed.

That is the theory.
No, that is the truth:
it's just so hard to grasp.
If God really does understand, we say –
if he really knows, feels how bad it is, my pain –
how can he let it be?
My God, how can you forsake me,
leave me to bear
this unbearable cross?
Your silence is the last straw.

And when I pray for my friend
and I see him get worse
and his faith begin to cloud over:
that, too, is pain.
God, can you understand that pain too?
The pain of your own seeming absence?
'My God, how can you forsake me . . .'

Jesus, made perfect through suffering.
Is suffering, then
the only route to perfection?

Suffering *is.*
That, for the moment, is the bottom line.
And God is showing us how everything,

including the black stuff,
is raw material for his new creation.
Raw. Yes. But how often
black conceals gold.

Suffering exhaustion
Jesus learns not to give in, to switch off, but to pray
and to trust his Father's agenda;
suffering thirst
he learns to look for God's unexpected solution
to save a Samaritan village;
suffering loss, of reputation, of friends
he learns to value the world's rewards
but hold them lightly;
suffering grief
he learns to love the image of God in a man
and forgive his frailty;
suffering the anguish of others' sin
he learns to deny himself
and take up his cross.

Suffering sets the scene
and points the need
for holiness.

And if Jesus,
then me. I, too,
must be made perfect through suffering.

I may not understand how my friend feels
but I must learn:
first to listen, to him and to my own pain;
then to let God move me
to realise my inadequacy,
and to trust him;
to plead with him to release compassion in me
to love for him;
to know my times are in his hands
and give myself generously;

to see with his eyes the devastation of sin
and fight harder, and with his weapons;
then to glimpse the Holy Spirit at work
and praise him!

And so to grow;
not just to feel, and suffer with my suffering friend
but grow in holiness
without which not one of us will see God.

Home and Dry

Jeremiah 31:7-14; Psalm 147:12-20; John I:10-18

When I left home that morning
the sun was shining,
I was young,
carrying little weight,
trusting the world
to be well-disposed towards one
who was well-disposed towards
the world.

I heard the forecast, warning
of mist over high ground;
I had faith,
though, that today was mine:
took stock
and stepped out,
climbing where map read
or fancy led.

Not long before rough ground
slowed me, eroded,
a little,
my confidence; forced
the detour, altered
the horizon: just as
the sun blanked
behind cloud.

A minute, and mist is all around.
God, are you there? Where?
I falter;
why does the world conspire,
weather against me?

I reap what others have sown,
see little now,
grow cold.

Why not like it was once before,
ambient light, as it were
from heaven
touching water
with white fire,
back-projecting colours of heaven
onto moorland earth:
oh, to hold it!
This, oh this finds the very core
of my being: moves me
to be still,
still . . .
or my slightest move
will remind me of feet still leashed to earth,
that evening comes, and I must
head home.

Because you called me Israel,
promised me milk and honey,
I didn't think
I would ever go hungry.
Because you called yourself shepherd
I didn't think
you would ever let me be hounded
across the earth.

Because you gave me your word
as a lamp to my feet
I didn't think
I would fall so often.
Because you are God Almighty
I didn't think
I'd be tempted so often
by second best.

I forgot that Israel wrestled with God,
that fighting came first
and feasting
followed faith.
I forgot that shepherds lead
but sheep must follow;
and wolves wait for
those who stray.

I forgot that I must choose
to take the light
of your word
and by it read, and obey.
I forgot that, unless I learn
to lift you in my heart above all else
I am lured by less
demanding loves.

Life may still be a bed of roses:
but East of Eden,
roses have thorns,
and black spot, and need to be pruned.
Gardeners sweat
as they fight for a brief summer
of fragrant flowers
and a long withering winter.

Life may still be a bowl of cherries
but East of Eden,
cherries fall
before they are ripe;
birds and insects peck and burrow,
damp induces mould
and we break our teeth
on the stones.

No, the road is rougher,
more circuitous, uncertain
than I thought;

the journey must be made
in all weathers, across
every type of terrain,
tasting exhaustion, brokenness
and such thirst –

but never despair,
because of the feast!
Guarantee
of God who does not lie;
we will be rescued by the one who sent the storm,
washed in his flood,
clothed by the one whose thorns tore us to shreds,
and spilled blood;

healed by the hands that broke
in order to mend; we will be seated
and treated
to such a feast only heaven could dream,
totally overwhelmed
by the goodness of God,
totally satisfied:
home.

But remember,
oh, remember! God's feast
may confound
my expectation: being not here, but there
where the first are last, and the last first;
I do not come home to the home I left.
And I must come weeping
to find joy.

Remember, oh Lord,
to grace me home; save me a place
at your feast.

Epiphany

Following Stars

Isaiah 60:1-6; Psalm 72:(1-9), 10-15; Ephesians 3:1-12; Matthew 2:1-12

Like surfers we stand
poised, trying to anticipate the next big wave

we all do it,
businesses looking for the untapped market
that will see them nicely through the next decade;
publishers hunting the next Booker prize winner
with several sequels up their sleeve;
clubbers spying out the next cool venue
where anyone who is anyone will go to be seen.

Whose star is in the ascendancy?
Keep up! or miss out . . .

we all do it,
head hunters second-guessing the skills of the future
capturing creativity;
media bosses plotting the rise and fall
of the market's idols;
politicians predicting what will save the nation
and win them the next election.

Whose star is in the ascendancy?
Keep up! or miss out . . .

But who is setting the pace? Who is calling the shots?
Do things simply happen, evolve, because life's like that
and we poor mortals just do our best to see round the next corner?
Or is someone, somewhere, pulling the strings,
playing with us like puppets, making us jump, and jumpy
as they move the goalposts, just for the hell of it?

Who says
that every High St fashion store will stock only minis and crop tops this
    year?
Designers' whim? Or hand in glove with the porn trade?
Who says
that the next thing to dominate the political agenda is the war on terror?
Necessity? Or cynical smokescreen, displacement tactics?
Who says
that there's no place for creation theory on the school curriculum?
True educationalists? Or a secular lobby?

Who says
that I must watch out for whose star is in the ascendancy,
that I must keep up, or miss out?

When the focus of the world's attention
is shifting, always shifting:
from the White House to Black Africa
from gold mines to oil wells
from priest to scientist
from Western Bloc to Pacific Rim
from kings and presidents to multi-nationals
from economic growth to climate change:

how am I to know,
how to read the signs, if I'm not to miss out?

how am I to know
on whom the mantle will next alight?

and how am I to know
whose star will still be shining when the final curtain falls?

But this I do know,
this: that when the planets cease to spin
and the tides of all the affairs of men recede
and the heavens stand, for a moment,
still: that the star will stand, there,
where it stood before: over the house of Israel

and over its most famous Son,
locus from which all life came
and to which all life must again come ...

The opposite of a *black hole*:
dazzling wholeness
drawing all things, all men and women to itself –
himself:
from east and west nations,
kings, sons and daughters,
herds of camels, fleets of ships and flights
of birds and planes;
wise men of every kind and gender,
those who knew, and those who thought
they didn't want to know,
mountains, trees and all creation –
not to swallow them up, use and discard them,
a passing craze, as is the way of the world –
no, but to welcome them, one and all,
inviting them to make their true, their final home
in the place of praise.

And this I also know
this: that we, the house of Israel, we, who follow the Son,
we are to hold our course:
we are to shine like stars over a storm-tossed sea
until that defining hour when the earth slows
and the world sees whose star is for ever in the ascendancy.

Faint Yet Pursuing

Isaiah 42:1-9; Matthew 3:13-17

What with so many people not looking where they're going,
the world is full of bruised and broken reeds:
the tramps and the trampled on,
pavement people, walked over, downtrodden,
passed by, passed over
for jobs, for homes, for food, for love and care;
finding it hard to hold their head high
or meet the eye of another who will turn away.

Others, too, who appear to stand straight and proud
but are in fact propped by this or that:
take the trappings,
health, wealth, the company car
the admiring, if not entirely disinterested circle, and inside
they, too, are bowed, bruised, broken;
finding it hard to acknowledge the wounds
they so artfully hide.

And so the bruised reed resonates
across the years, since we persist
in battering one another,
and being battered
by the world, the flesh and the devil;
heart, mind, body, spirit –
who is there who has not suffered grief
in one or other?

And, in our own economy, we know
the bruised fruit is discarded,
the battered car written off,
the broken china binned;

what, then, of us, bruised and broken reeds?
And is the scrap-heap so bad, after all?
Is it worth the effort, to carry on?
Why not be invalided out?

And the smouldering wick:
so few, it seems, struggling
to shield the flame of faith
against the cold winds of competing doctrines,
seeing the opposition's headlines blaze
and the minds of the masses catch the fire
that will one day consume
while we trim our wicks in vain.

You tell us, Jesus, our light should shine
like a city set on a hill, a beacon;
that out of our hearts rivers
of living water should flow;
that others should look at us and marvel
at how we love one another . . . I fear
the bruised reed and the smouldering wick
describe me better.

And I'd fear, oh I would fear
how the Lord would deal
with such faulty and faithless servants
with such bruised and battered servants
with such hobbled and half-hearted servants
with such lame and light-under-a-bushel servants
were it not for that other,
dear, suffering Servant . . .

I can scarcely believe the graciousness of God
who comes, to accommodate
my brokenness and flickering faith;

who comes, working silently like yeast
to raise the world to heights of justice:
a quiet revolution

which gathers up its ragtag army,
binding up the broken and the broken-hearted,
fanning my fading faith,

refusing to let me go, because God who makes,
mends; God who loves me,
will not leave me: all is redeemable!

A bruised reed he will not break,
and a smouldering wick
he will not snuff out.

And this is *good news*, oh such good news!
That the word to me is *hope:*
I fail, yes, but I am not a failure;
neither have I undermined God's plan.
Hope is not the desperate last recourse
of a drowning man, but getting up
and setting my course, sure
of reaching home;

and this is *good news*, oh such good news!
That the word to me is *trust:*
however many times they've let me down,
my friends, my family, my boss
myself, the system –
there is still one who cannot but be true,
finally true: who has told me,
surely, he will see me home;

and this is *good news*, oh such good news!
That the word to me is *persevere:*
Lord, I cannot cope with this pain!
Lord, I cannot bring up this child on my own!
Lord, I cannot stand the pressure of this job!
Lord, I cannot ever pay this debt!
Yet you say, 'Get up! I am gentle with the poor,
and I have promised you a kingdom . . .'

And so I will keep coming, Lord,
for as long as there is heaven, there is hope of heaven;
I will keep coming, Lord,
for as long as you have faith in me, I surely have faith in you;
I will keep coming, Lord,
bruised, battered, torn, tattered,
mud-spattered saint and pardoned sinner,
faint but pursuing – I will come.

The Perfect Church

1 Corinthians 1:1-9

If you find it,
don't join it – you'll spoil it,

as the saying goes;
but perhaps it ain't as simple as that?

True,
churches are where
we sinners become more aware of each other's failings
(if not of our own)
and it is hard to think of each other as saints
knowing, as we do,
the elevation of the trivial over the important,
the nailing of reputations to the notice board
along with the flower rota
the gossip column and the fifth column,
the casual commodification of God.

So why, as so many suggest,
can't we get back to doing things like they did
in the New Testament church?
Take Corinth, for example.

Oh –
hang on a minute.
Perhaps not *Corinth* . . .

Corinth,
full of cliques, snobbishness
and brazen immorality;
hazy on doctrine, lazy on discipline,

thumbing the nose at authority;
enjoying the glamour, the clamour
of new-found gifts, the soulishness
of litigation and lack of love.

Only a few years, and they'd gone astray,
the young Christians:
but in this ragbag, rootless, ruthless city
perhaps we should hesitate
as much to blame
as to imitate.

Nevertheless,
I guess you'll have a few words to say, Paul:
let them have it with both barrels!

But what is this?

Paul, are you insane?
Has all your hardship and suffering
not only damaged your sight
but softened your brain?
Why do you greet this shameful Church
with words of gratitude and grace,
anticipation and delight?

You celebrate grace given
though you see it spurned, misunderstood, abused;
you praise the gift of godly speech
though you hear self-glorifying babble;
you marvel at their knowledge
though you have to take them back to basics;
you are happy that they lack nothing,
that they're well on the way to being
the perfect church ??

Paul, are you falling prey to the power
of positive thinking? Wishful thinking? Or merely confused?
Or could it be
that you see with God's eyes?

You write, after all, not to *your* church,
the one you founded, taught, agonised over
but to the *church of God* which is at Corinth:
every one whom God, not you, has called;
every one whom Christ, not you, has justified;
every one to whom the Spirit, not you, has imparted life –
every one whom God has
stirred by love
called by name
freed from shame
saved to serve
told they are but little lower than angels, and the whole
of heaven is theirs for the asking . . .
In Christ
all things are not only possible
but accomplished
for all eternity; Corinth stands resplendent in the presence of God
because his will and calling cannot fail:
he is faithful . . .

All, then, that remains to do,
Corinth, is to work out your salvation here and now,
in fear and trembling,
for it is God who works in you, and I, Paul
see with the eye of faith
how he makes his dreams of a perfect church come true.

Oh –
hang on a minute.
If Corinth – then why not us, even us?

Paul, could you ever greet my shameful church
with words of such gratitude and grace,
anticipation and delight?
See that despite our careless talk, gossip and compromise
God has planted seeds of bold speech, encouragement
and soft answers that defuse anger?
See that despite our undistinguished living
God has given us power, and love, and self-control
and a call to light up the world?

See that despite our apathy and ignorance and fear
God has transferred the wealth of his wisdom
into our account?

Paul, can you see with the eye of faith
how he makes his dream of a perfect church come true
here, now, even
in *my* church?

If I could believe that,
maybe I wouldn't feel so much like giving up;
if I could see with the eye of faith,
the eye of God, maybe I could
reflect with gratitude
act with grace
pray with anticipation
dance with delight:
hold on, hope ever renewed
at the sure prospect
of all that your faithfulness will unfold:

the perfect church
one day:
yes!

Party Animals

1 Corinthians 1:10-18

'Of course, it's not the same as when Father Michael was here . . .
He taught me everything I know,
heard my confession twice a year,
and oh, his voice was so soft and low;

the two we've had since, and the one now
well, I dare say they do their best, but it's not the same;
one wore trainers, and didn't bow
and this one's female, though she's not to blame

so we still go, most Sundays when it's dry
and when it's not that noisy 'People's Praise'
but me and my friends, we always wonder why
it can't be like it was in the good old days

and so we sit together in our pews and reminisce
and think what Father Michael would have done,
commemorate the one we love and miss
our father in the faith, and each of us his son

and we pray, Our Father . . .'

'Of course, it's not as good when Dr Cleverly's not there;
pleasant enough, but light-weight,
baby food: we need more solid fare
than the ice-cream on offer at the fête,

and he has acquired such great learning:
we count ourselves extremely blessed
to sit at his feet, our hearts burning,
digging deep into the Bible's treasure chest;

God surely meant that we should use our brains,
not park them at the church door;
but most will settle for a few grains
when God, and Dr Cleverly, can offer so much more!

and so we follow him around the town
take notes, discuss, increase our understanding;
perhaps, occasionally, look down
on those whose intellectual thirst is less demanding

  but we pray, Our Father . . .'

'Of course, it's not the same when we ignore tradition
laid down, over many years, like good wine;
not that we want to be in competition
but surely we must draw the line

when all that long-established discipline
of prayer and practice, bricks and mortar
of our faith, is lightly tossed into the bin,
baby out with bath-water

to make way for the new, improved
post-modern culture-friendly brand;
we fear the goalposts have been moved
too far: this house is built on sand;

my friends and I, we'll fly the flag,
keep to the book and sing the old songs;
it's true, wild horses will not drag
us out from where we know the truth belongs

  but we pray, Our Father . . .'

'Of course, it's not the same when men and women lead,
for we can go direct to God;
has he not promised that he'll feed
us, guide us with his staff, and check us with his rod?

My friends and I, we have no need
of go-betweens, of prophet or of priest,
Peter, Paul, Apollos, or the modern breed
of guru, be they from the west or east;

we have the Spirit of God who speaks straight to our soul;
we have the promise of God to claim
we have the Word of God, his whole
counsel: we pray in the power of Jesus' name,

so why should we need any other head?
Perhaps we should come apart
and be free to follow where Christ has led,
give ourselves a fresh start

   but we pray, Our Father . . .'

We'll all pray Our Father, as we've been taught –
but what a dysfunctional family we present!
Forgetting it was Christ who brought
us life, bought us life, we resent

those who would depose our favourite figurehead
who fail to see the rightness of our way
and so we go where angels fear to tread:
off into cliques and factions, where we still pray

Our Father, deaf to our own hypocrisies
that brother turns his back on brother,
and sisters lack the common courtesies:
see how these Christians hurt one another . . .

Jesus, the prayer torn from the depths of your being
was that we, your fractious family, might be one
might recognise the many modes of God, seeing
that discord dishonours, and harmony beats unison:

and so we pray, Our Father, forgive us
        partisan,
        party animals;
        Jesus, keep us
        at the foot of the cross
        looking only to you;
        Spirit, grace us
        with warmth and humility
        to embrace others.

At My Wits' End

1 Kings 17:8-16; 1 Corinthians 1:18-31

I do believe that God is everywhere
but it's usually at my wits' end
that I find him

that's if, finally resorting to prayer,
I recognise him
for his ways are not mine.

I mean, if you were God, and had a hungry prophet on your hands,
wouldn't you line up a widow with wealth enough and to spare?
But no. Instead of choosing one who had it in their power to help
he goes out of his way to find one whose cupboard was bare.

Perhaps, when you have nothing, there is more space for a miracle
                                        less for independence

I mean, if you were Elijah, looking for promised hospitality,
wouldn't you ignore the poor widow looking for sticks, sure
that she cannot be the one? But no. Instead of falling back on reason
he takes God at his word and looks no further.

Perhaps, with reason submitted, there is more space for faith
                                        less for judgement

I mean, if you were the widow and about to starve to death,
wouldn't you question the gall of a God who asks you to take in a guest?
But no. Instead of protesting her own necessity
she gives her two mites of oil and flour, at whatever cost.

Perhaps at our wits' end, there is more space for trust
                                        less for calculation.

But we are so keen
to maintain our independence
to execute judgement
to calculate our own comfort.
And so our local project foundered for want of anyone willing
to offer the workers a home;
they might have come in late,
played loud music
been fussy with their food
wanted to have friends to stay
made free with the internet
left socks on the radiators
and half-eaten pot-noodle in the loo –
and anyway, we needed the spare room for Auntie's annual visit;
but hey, although for all we know
Elijah snored
he saved their lives, the widow and her son
not once, but twice.
Why can't we take God at his word,
open the door to trust, to faith,
to miracle?
Why must we come to our wits' end
before we will
risk?

The Bible, after all, is brimful of encouragement.
'We've no food, so let's invite 5000 people to dinner.'
'We have a sacrifice to burn and no fire, so let's soak it with water first.'
'We have an incurable leper, so let's tell him to wash in the river.'
'We have an impossible city to take, so let's walk round and play trumpets.'
'We've no more wine, so let's offer washing water instead.'
'We have a man born blind, so let's put mud on his eyes.'
Glorious experiment!
that says 'Why resign yourself to the inevitable
when it's only your resignation that makes it inevitable?'
When the God of cause and effect can nevertheless
confound our expectations,
surprise us again

into worship and wonder
that he, the first cause
is not to be limited in his effects . . .

There are times
when we must leave our logic,
park our reason
and accept the divine non sequitur
which follows
only the optimism and the obedience of faith . . .

but Lord, may they not only be the times
I am at my wits' end:

I want to learn your multiplication table
not just when my cupboard is bare
but because I share freely the daily bread
which is still your miracle;
I want to learn such complete surrender
not just when little else appeals
but always: that fire from heaven may burn up
my complacency;
I want to learn how to be divinely whole
not just when disease is apparent
but through and through
from the inside out;
I want to learn how to gain ground
not just when a major enemy threatens
but over the little daily skirmishes with fear
and lack of love;
I want to learn how to celebrate
not just when you sign your name
but amazed at *every* good gift
reflecting your grace;
I want to learn how to see
not heaven from earth,
but earth from heaven, day to day, as you see,
mud and stars.

As Paul knew he should not trust
in his considerable learning
but only in Christ and him crucified:
so must I be turning
not to my wispy wits
but to him who takes miracles in his stride

that I may find the God who is everywhere
surprising me.

Ordinary Time

Life in the Fast Lane

Isaiah 58:1-9a (9b-12); Psalm 112:1-9 (10); 1 Corinthians 2:1-12 (13-16);
Matthew 5:13-20

'I'm sorry,' I said 'but I'm not overtaking.
It's raining; I've only just got used to driving on the other side
and they're all going much too fast.
I'll just find a nice lorry and tuck in behind it.'

'Fine as a survival tactic when visiting your twin town,' he said,
'but it just won't do as a philosophy for life.

'Christians, you know, are called to live in the fast lane.'

'Lord?'

'Fast. Prayer and fasting. Sometimes it's the only way.'

'Oh Lord! That kind of fast doesn't come easy, either,
to one for whom food is one of life's greatest pleasures.
Must I?
Didn't you say to Isaiah, and to the Pharisees,
they'd got it all wrong about fasting?'

'Hang on! It's not quite as simple as that.
The Pharisees thought they'd cracked it:
a few great fast days, plus Mondays and Thursdays
if you were really serious; and if there was an 'r' in the month
or the wind was blowing from the south-east
or you chanced to have brushed against a dead body –
fast, to be on the safe side; one has to agree
they dotted every 'i', crossed every 't';

'credit where credit's due: they knew the letter of the law,
bound it to head and hand; for the most part

were dutiful in the observance – but precisely as a matter
of head and hand: not of the heart.'

'That's what I mean, Lord;
what you want is not the absence of food
but the presence of good deeds
born of love!'

'True. So, how are you doing?'

'Ah. Little bit of love, little bit of duty
and, if I'm honest
quite a bit of tucking in behind the nearest lorry
and keeping my head down.'

'Because you're not keen on the fast lane.'

'No, Lord. No, I'm not keen on the fast lane.
And what's the point?
You said yourself, it's not going without food
but giving without measure.'

'That's right; those are the real deeds of power,
deeds which provoke others to praise me:
deeds prompted not by obedience to the law
but inspired and powered by the Holy Spirit,

'deeds with a flavour, a light, a fragrance
which hint at heaven.'

'Easier said than done, Lord.'

'Indeed. But unless what's said can be translated
into what's done, what do you have but the hollow form
of godliness? Words forming a frame
but no picture.

'Do you remember? "In the beginning, God *said*" – the Word.
Just one Word; that was enough.

But the Word I spoke was made up not of letters, but love
and so the Word became flesh and walked into your life
and you saw, and touched, and knew how my love felt
and that you were called, not to describe
but to bear my love, tough, tender, extreme:
to shock the world, now as then . . .

'A world where there are too many words
which are not being made flesh;
for my people choose the slipstream of the world
over the fast lane . . .'

'Well, Lord: if you tell me to fast, I suppose I must do it;
but what if my heart isn't in it?
Then I am no better than a noisy gong – or Pharisaic cymbal;
no good will come of it.'

'I do not tell you to fast; I do not want you
to obey an order, and end up with an empty ritual.
But I think you will find yourself fasting
when you no longer want to be full of empty words;
when you no longer want to be full of selfish genes;
when you no longer want to be full of the world's wisdom;
when the fact that your heart isn't in it
brings you to your knees.

'And then you'll not *decide* to fast
but rather recognise that your resource is not enough;
desire for wisdom, guidance, love – for God himself
will fill your being, and for that time nothing
will distract, for nothing else will satisfy,
and you will not let go of me
until I bless you with all you need
to live in the fast lane.'

The Other Side of the Coin

Deuteronomy 30:15-20

Bless my soul!
I never realised there was another side to the coin:
that, if I so choose –
or, failing to choose the best,
favour the worst –
then my soul may be not blessed, but cursed.
Strange how our brains refuse the words we'd rather not hear.

'This day I call heaven and earth to witness
that I have set before you
life and death,
blessings and curses.
Now choose life,
so that you and your children may live . . .'

Come on, Moses –
who in their right mind wouldn't choose life,
and blessings?
That's an easy box to tick.

But hang on – there's something else here,
an uncomfortable thought:
it would appear
that *God* not only blesses
but curses. God?!
Not, of course, in the sense of using bad language
of cussing and swearing at the soaring phone bill when the kids are home,
or when the sale falls through –
but in the sense of establishing, and spelling out
cause and effect:
faith and obedience bring blessing: that's how it is,

that is the measure for which we are made,
that is to choose life;
but ignoring the word, and rejecting the love of God
bring judgement: that's how it is,
that is as far as our own road leads,
that is to choose death.

And I must make the choice once and for all
and I must make the choice many times a day
and I must make the choice for myself alone
and I must make the choice knowing that generations to come will pay.
And I must make the choice aware that *my* words can bless
and I must make the choice aware that *my* words can curse
and I must make the choice aware that all of my words and acts,
by the will of God, will affect our lives, for better or worse.

The trouble is,
words slip
and I dare say Satan has a vested interest
in grooming those that might otherwise
blow his disguise.
'Curse' for most of us implies
full-blown witchcraft, pins in effigies or spells,
something medieval, lingering only in the Lady of Shallott,
Voodoo ritual or suspect fairy tales.
No wonder, then, we do not realise
the supernatural power at work within the words, or recognise
the fatal signs.

'Of course, heart problems run in the family,
so I don't stand much chance!'
'Everything always seems to happen to her –
she's just accident-prone.'
Curses.
'They seem fated
never to make a go of a business . . . '
'You'll never succeed as a teacher,
you're too much of an introvert.'
Curses!

'I always told him, he'd end up in prison:
weak, just like his father.'
'She vowed she'd never, ever,
trust a man again.'
Curses!

Curses.
Some would call it negative confession,
and talk about the power of positive thinking:
but it's more than that.
My words convey more than the force field
of my opinion, even of my own spirit; whether I know it or not,
I tune in to a higher – or lower – frequency
and bless
or curse
myself
or others.

'I always go to the fortune teller at the fête –
but only for a bit of fun.'
'Well, of course you would be a worrier:
you're Gemini, aren't you?'
Curses.
'His dad was quite high up in one of those secret orders:
but it's all about charity, really.'
'She swears by these crystals,
says she hasn't had a migraine since.'
Curses!
'My dad was such a bully, a control freak;
I haven't spoken to him for years.'
'It's a real swinging neighbourhood,
but they're all really nice people, you know.'
Curses!

Curses.
Some would call it spirituality,
being a free spirit, finding what works for you.
But it's less than that.
My actions convey more than a personal whim;
whether I know it or not

I express a higher – or lower – calling
and honour
or betray
God
or devil . . .

devil,
who does not, himself, curse:
but delights to mislead us into the dark side of God,
where disobedience delivers us to death.

But bless our God of grace!
who, in Christ, took every curse
and, hanging on the cross-tree
himself nailed
the reckoning for rebellion
and, rising, flipped the coin:
heads
for blessing,
Christ the Head,
cutting us free from every curse
that would keep us from blessing
and being blessed.

Bless my soul!
And bless the Lord, my soul!

Take Two

Leviticus 19:1-2, 9-18; Matthew 5:38-48

'The rain it raineth every day
upon the just and unjust fella;
but mainly on the just, because
the unjust took the just's umbrella.'

And if the just is to justify himself as a true Christian gentleman,
he will catch up with the unjust, offer to reimburse his bus fare
and take him home for tea.

Such is the limitless love of God
and we are called to be perfect, as he is perfect.

Have you heard it said,
'Do not hold back the wages of a hired man overnight',
all you superstores, big businesses who never pay your small suppliers
till the last possible moment?
How about cash on the nail,
or even a small investment as a mark of loyalty, a vote of confidence?

But without the limitless love of God
alive in us
we will never be perfect, as he is perfect.

At most, I will be fair, pay on time
the required amount
and maybe a bonus at Christmas;
to do more would be to jeopardise my own financial security;
    to allow my heart to rule my head;
        to refuse to shut my eyes to the stress and struggle of others . . .

to do more would be –
to be Christ-like.

Have you heard it said,
'Do not go about spreading slander among your people',
all you columnists and chat show hosts who exchange gossip
as your common currency?
How about a moratorium on rumour
or even some words of praise for unsung heroes?

But without the limitless love of God
alive in us
we will never be perfect, as he is perfect.

At most I will check my sources
and confine myself to what is true,
if not always kind or necessary.
To do more would be to risk a drop in circulation;
    to allow morality to clip the wings of marketing;
        to refuse to sanction ruin, to promote restoration . . .

to do more would be –
to be Christ-like.

Have you heard it said,
'Do not deceive one another',
all you who disguise your predatory motives in lavish promises
and very small print?
How about safeguarding
the other man's interests, looking even to bless him?

But without the limitless love of God
alive in us
we can never be perfect, as he is perfect.

At most I will promise no more
and no less than I can deliver:
no hidden extras.
To do more would be to lose out to my competitors;
    to allow grace to replace greed;
        to refuse to take advantage of the less streetwise . . .

to do more would be –
to be Christ-like.

As for me – I have heard it said,
'Love your neighbour as yourself',
but I have chosen my neighbourhood with care;
and although I know that Jesus
also told me to love my enemies
I kid myself I have no enemies,
conveniently skipping over those who come between:
   those home and alone, who long for more than a friendly 'Good
      morning';
   those who graffiti the walls, who need more than my disapproval;
   those who walk the streets for reasons I assume and pre-judge;
   those who would try to undermine and rubbish my faith;
   those with whom I think I have little in common: but do I know?
   those who live in *that* street, on *that* side of the river, who go to *that* pub –
   who are probably thinking exactly the same about me –
Do I know?
Do I care?
Do I see the image of God
in them, no more distorted,
no less redeemable than it is in me?
Do I dare to admit that my lack of love
is one of the things that binds them
as it binds me?

But without the limitless love of God
alive in me
I can never be perfect, as he is perfect.

At most I will be known
for my moderate charity,
my customary fairness, my small kindnesses;
but where, oh where in me is that
unfailing generosity
habitual warmth, breadth of vision?
Where the shocking disregard
for my rights, my self-interest,
society's approval ratings?
Where the refusal
to count the cost?

True love,
Christ's love, does not calculate:
there is no debate.
Christ's love sees, hears, acts
and the world is unmade

and remade.

Lent

Chicken and Egg

Genesis 1:1–2:3

That old chestnut,
you know, the one about 'Which came first,
the chicken or the egg?'
Well, I've cracked it!
Obvious, really, when you come to think about it.
I mean, it has to be the chicken, doesn't it?
Because the egg wouldn't hatch on its own,
and if it did,
the chick would find no food, or the wrong food,
or fall foul of the fox,
and if it didn't,
well, without another chicken
that particular bit of natural history would pretty soon be
just history
and none of us would be able
to go to work on an egg.

Neither can I imagine
that God wouldn't have come up with a fully-fledged design,
not just some shell of an idea.
No, I can't imagine God,
like some medieval alchemist,
watching anxiously to see what manner of fish, flesh or fowl
will emerge from this particular egg:
from the beginning,
God created
out of the blue
out of a clear blue sky
out of the blueprints which tumbled,
endlessly, it seems,
from his divine invent-ory.

Yes, God created!
He saw all that he had made,
and it was not a confused, cruel and wasteful experiment,
trial and error, sorting out the mess
from the explosion in the laboratory
but a *fait accompli*
by one who knew what he wanted,
one who saw, not the possibility of *chicken*
after a few millennia of featherweight failures
but cock and hen, triumphantly greeting the dawn
from day one
(OK, day five if you *will* be pedantic)
however long that day may have been.

Yes, God created!
Every creature according to its kind . . .
Darwin, to be fair,
was well aware of the fault lines in his own theory;
that if any complex creature
could not have evolved one step at a time
without starving, falling prey, drowning, blowing away
or otherwise foundering
then his theory also foundered. Hey ho!
   for spiders
   bombardier beetles
   sea slugs
   butterflies
   etc., etc.
oh, and those amazing penguins!
Not black and white animated cartoons:
more like extreme sports,
pre-programmed
with the painful love and persistence
of their creator.

Yes, God created!
If only I'd been famous enough

to do the magazine interview
and be asked 'What do *you* think is the best invention ever?'
I wouldn't have hesitated.
Trees.
Can you imagine a world without trees?
Deserts would multiply,
villages drown,
the whole ecological system break down;
no logs for cabins, no rafters for roofs
no charcoal for artists, no paper for books
no nuts for squirrels, no apples, no pears
no rubber or resin, no climbing the stairs
no willow for cricket, no nesting for birds:
no boats in the harbour, too barren for words . . .
But God
had this uniquely beautiful idea
to shelter, breathe, provide, sustain
and spoke the word:
tree,
in its thousand incarnations
pre-programmed
with the nurturing love and regeneration
of its creator.

Tree
not indeterminate seed;
fish
not roe;
chicken
not unprotected egg;
man
not some spare hydrogen atoms which might,
over slow millennia and against all the odds grow
into some kind of upmarket monkey –
and woman
at just the same time
or yet another species would have been extinct
before it even got off the ground.

Yes, God created!
We cannot create
tree or leaf, seed or flower, fruit, root or blade of grass
animal, vegetable, mineral, chicken or egg:
nothing, in fact;
only mix and modify, separate, accelerate and synthesise,
catalyse, cross-fertilise
and claim the credit
for glory that belongs to God.
Not for him the painful space
between imagining and execution,
the wrong notes, smudged canvas, crossings out;
enough to speak the word
for vision to materialise,
for love which must be shared
to overflow, and overwhelm our world
with wonders.

It completely defeats me
how anyone can seriously believe
that our beautiful, intricate, world
happened by chance

or, if they do,
why they haven't made of chance
a god.

Let Me Make Up Your Mind

Exodus 24:12-18; 2 Peter 1:16-21

They tell me, I am what I eat: maybe.
More important, I am what – or who –
I choose to listen to.

I am, after all, brainwashed. We all are,
in this age of death by communication.
It just depends what brand of washing soap we choose.

Who do we listen to?
Which bands, solo artist, rapper?
Do we go for the beat, or does the philosophy also seduce us?

Who do we listen to?
Our parents, grandparents – though we'd never admit it –
or the wisdom of the school gate?

Who do we listen to?
The newspaper that reflects our prejudices?
The magazine that feeds our fantasies?

Who do we listen to?
Pop psychology from the agony aunt?
Or select from a range of self-help gurus on the shelf?

Who do we listen to?
Our doctor, teacher, lawyer,
friend, mentor, counsellor, vicar – God (whoever he may be)?

Who do we listen to?
Or don't we really know
who to listen to?

When wave upon wave of words
breaks on us – threatens to overwhelm us –
which voice speaks with authority?

When we are wired up to music
like anaesthetic, deadening the brain,
whose note rings clear and true above the rest?

When the air is woven thick
with text and trivia, webbed to catch the unwary,
who deserves to be heard?

Who do we listen to?
No, *really* listen to –
or don't we really know any more
who to listen to?
Have we mortgaged our mind
to the highest bidder?

Peter was in no doubt
about who is worthy of our attention
and who is not.

We are awash with cleverly invented stories,
both fact and fiction, but unless they chime
with the greatest story ever told, beware them:

listen, says Peter, to the prophets
for God has spoken through them
and history proved them true;

listen, he says, to us, the apostles
for we were there, and we saw and heard for ourselves
and tell what we know to be true;

listen, he says, to Jesus the Son
for God put his finger on him and said 'This is the One:
listen to him; he is full of grace and truth.'

Yes, that was then
and we are here, and today,
but authority rests in the same revelation of God:

Old and New Testaments,
prophets, historians, poets, apostles and the Spirit of Jesus
calling across the years: listen to him!

Listen! for he alone has the big picture
and he alone sees, hears, understands you;
and he alone weaves the two together, as if you were made for each other.

Listen! for he will light you, delight you;
listen! for he will fire you, inspire you;
listen! if, indeed, you have not forgotten how to listen . . .

Real listening
engages the brain as well as the ears,
alerts the imagination
and awakens the will.
It is not just a case of sound waves playing across the synapses
but of my rising to meet the challenge of what I hear.

It is no light task, listening;
I mean, it took Moses forty days and forty nights
to get his head round the Ten Commandments.

But me? In one ear and out the other;
but if I am not changed by what I hear,
then I have not heard.

If something has not changed between us,
then I have not listened to the other:
I have only heard words
and I fear that often
the art of conversation is dead
because the art of listening has died;

and if we find it so hard
truly to listen to one another
how much harder, Lord, to hear your voice

not simply as words of wisdom from a bygone age
but as words that leap from the page
immediate as the latest email;

words that slip into our minds unsought
but with an edge of excitement
and a ring of truth,

words seeking not just a listening ear
for a moment, but our full attention
and steps of faith and obedience.

Who do we listen to?
Choose carefully, for you are letting them
make your mind up for you.

Just Looking

Genesis 2:15-17, 3:1-7; Matthew 4:1-11

She must have seen it before,
the tree in the middle of the garden;
walked past it every day, I dare say,
sat in its shade and played I spy with Adam.
But that's as far as it went:
knowing it to be forbidden fruit
she gave it not another thought,
not another glance –

till the serpent came and said 'Look!
Just look! Did you ever see
such a beautiful bloom on such soft skin,
such a sunset palette of subtle shades,
such tautness, straining for touch
of lips and teeth. Look, just look!
Such a feast for the senses,
foretaste of heaven!'

And so she looked,
allowed that look to linger,
to unlock imagination,
admit lust, and lies:
to lock out love's echo
'Just don't go there . . . !'

Just looking.
That's all she was doing. Just looking.
But that was enough.

He knew he didn't need
another music magazine; but Smith's
looked bright, and warm, and inviting

on the cold February day,
and soon he was running his eye
along the shelf, thinking, not
'Just looking!' nor even 'Shall I? Should I?'
but 'Which one?'

And, well, you know how
one thing leads to another;
in the sports section, there's one
with a wall chart of the champions' league.
What else? His roving eye
reaches the top shelf,
lingers . . . Somehow, he slips
a third paper between the other two.

Just looking.
That's all he was doing. Just looking.
But that was enough.

The letter was addressed to her
by name, so she read it
and the pictures on the leaflet
held her eye: the palm-lined beach,
the keys for the new car,
the laptop and the free, slim-line
mobile phone when you signed up
for the loan.

And, well, you know how
one thing leads to another;
instead of thinking 'Hold on!
I've already got my student loan to pay back!'
she tells herself 'It's the only way
I'll ever get these things before I'm too old
to enjoy them; in for a penny, in for a pound!
Enjoy it now, sort it later.'

Just looking.
That's all she was doing. Just looking.
But that was enough.

And Jesus, when the enemy
tempted him to turn stones into bread –
did he let his eyes linger
on the rock-strewn desert
and think 'Wow! Just imagine,
if only all these were warm, fragrant
crusty loaves: why,
I could feed the world!

'And they would come to me,
they would worship me
because of my care for them
and my miraculous touch.
And in any case, right now
I could use a loaf or two myself,
build up my strength
to fight the enemy . . .'

Or did he know that just looking
is the beginning of the end,
listen then to the voice of his father,
'Just don't go there!'
close his eyes
and tell the devil to get lost?

To refuse to go there,
to refuse even to look
is not the escapist's way
but the only way to resist temptation.

If my eye offends me,
sends me into forbidden territory –
well, sell the TV,
cut up my credit card,
take myself off the mailing list,
set up a standing order to charity
and remember not to shop
when I'm feeling hungry!

Never mind if it's a case of sin
or simply making the most
of my time, money, emotional energy,
making the most of the time because the days are evil.
Either way, it's a case
of not needing to go there,
nor to be worldly-wise; of being content
with a kind of innocence;

the kind Eve lost
through the lust of the eye:
by just looking.

Fathers and Sons: Drama in Three Acts

Genesis 12:1-4a; Romans 4:1-5, 13-17

Cast: Abraham (Ab), Moses (Mo), Referee (Ref), Cast of Thousands (C of T), Abraham United (AU), Moses Wanderers (MW)

Act 1

Ref   In the blue corner: our veteran champion, travelled, tried and tested! One or two defeats, but some remarkable victories, and the promise of more to come! Let's hear it for Big Daddy Abraham! *(C of T oblige)*

And in the red corner: our persistent challenger; a few struggles since that dramatic beginning, but emerging now from his wilderness period and sticking to that punishing training schedule. Let's hear it for Mountain Man Moses! *(C of T)* Seconds away!

Mo   C'mon then, Abe – you're flabby! Anyone would think your God doesn't stand for anything; he's a push-over!

Ab   You know that's not true! Anyone would think *your* God was a tyrant – laying down the law like that.

Mo   He has a right to! The designer has the right to tell you how the thing works, you know. *Don't put diesel in this engine . . .* If we want God to protect us, prosper us, we must play by the rules.

Ab   That's not what he told me. He just told me to get up and go, follow where he led. So I got up and went. Easy! No – not easy: but simple. He called it faith – listening, and doing what he said. And that was fine by him: I was accepted! Nothing about lots of rules and regulations. Why do you guys always think you can improve on the original?

Mo   And why do you guys always think nothing should change? Nothing wrong with product development. Maybe we needed more to go on – needed to know the kind of thing he would be saying to us, you know, in case our hearing wasn't too good.

	You need to know the rules before you can play the game, after all: what's wrong with that?
Ab	Two things. I begin to lose sight of my God and see only the rule book: that makes me feel desolate. And I begin to see that I can't keep the rules: that makes me feel hopeless.
Mo	But that's how it is: the glory and the holiness of God would destroy us – believe me, I've been there. Like fire devouring dead leaves. That's why we have priests, go-betweens; and sacrifice, to deal with guilt.
Ab	I know all about sacrifice; I had a son . . . but when God speaks – that is enough.
Mo	You were privileged. Remember, he speaks also to the untaught and the deaf. I have it in writing. From him. So there!

Act 2

Ref	As the years went by, the sons of Abraham and the sons of Moses drew up their battle lines, and many a skirmish took place in arenas up and down the land. Abraham United versus Moses Wanderers: friendly match, but below the surface . . .
MW	We keep the rules, score the goals, work our way up the league table.
AU	Chill, man – we'll all get there in the end.
MW	We play charity matches, auction our shirts, haven't had a red card all season.
AU	Get you!
MW	In short, we live decent lives, keep our hands off other footballers' wives and feed the neighbours' cat.
AU	Admirable! (aside) Holy Joes . . .
MW	Regular weekend training sessions, midweek warm-ups, rule-book revision: if anyone deserves that cup, it's Moses Wanderers!
AU	Ref, was that not an own-goal?
Ref	Indeed.
MW	Eh?
Ref	Your number 11. Pride. It's against the rules.

MW	Well, it'll be the only goal you'll get: you're not even trying. You're a disgrace to the game.
AU	You try too hard. Love God, and do what you will. Hey, that's a good line – someone ought to make use of it.
MW	You're in cloud cuckoo land; no one can win the cup except by keeping the rules. God is a God of justice.
AU	You're stuck in the mud. This is a charity match, not a competition: and we're thecharity. God is a God of mercy.
MW	Idle scroungers!
AU	Teacher's pets!

Act 3

Ref	As time went on, the playing field became more and more confused. Many who wore the colours of Abraham United repeatedly scored own goals, behaving like a fifth column of Moses Wanderers; and most of the crowd decided that this was what the game was all about. To be a footballer was to be a Mountain Man Moses man; to be a Christian was to be someone who tried to keep the rules.
	Me? Well, of course I see both sides of the game. Abe! Moses! Let me tell you about someone who said, 'If you love me, you'll keep my commandments . . .'
Ab	There you are! It's all about love!
Mo	There you are! It's all about rules!
Ref	Will you listen? It's about both.
Ab/Mo	There you are! Oh . . .
Ref	Which comes first?
Ab	Love . . . first God loves me and gives me a place in heaven. Just because he loves me. Heaven knows why – no one deserves it. That's why I love him . . .
Ref	Exactly. Keeping the rules doesn't make him love you any more or any less; he loves you because he is love, and he loved you into existence.
Mo	But the rules – *he* gave the rules?

Ref   Only to show us how far we all are from the kingdom of heaven. A chapter: not the end of the story. In the end, it was sacrifice. Another son. His.

Ab   Knowing that . . . makes me want to be like him. Keep the rules . . .

Mo   But for love of him, not duty . . .

Ref   *Now* will you shake hands?

Eau de Vie

Exodus 17:1-7; John 4:5-42

Strange, that for the French
'water of life' is a spirit;
perhaps they know something we don't!
For Jesus, too, knew that the water of life
would course through our veins like brandy,
fiery Spirit reviving fainting souls . . .

Earth, air, fire – and water,
essential elements.
(I'll bet none of us has given up water for Lent.)

Water!
Scientists know
that life could not have begun, could not go on
without you; know
that they themselves are two-thirds H_2O, would die in days
without you; know
that you are a common, yet curious element:
pages of diagrams and formulae
chart your idiosyncrasies, each designed, it seems,
to further our well-being – yet your origin
escapes them.
(I can just imagine you looking over their shoulder, Lord,
as they scratch their heads, smiling and thinking
'Yes, it *was* rather ingenious!')

Where, indeed, would you have sprung from
if not the simple overflow of divine love?

Just a couple of bits of hydrogen
and a bit of oxygen

and rain falls
eyes blink
fish swim
children drink
boats sail
plants grow
food cooks
rivers flow
and our planet, blessed above all,
springs to life.

Earth, air, fire – and water,
essential elements.
These things belong to God: are in his gift
(not floated on the Stock Exchange, nor for sale on Ebay:
down with water privatisation, I say,
and charging for air at the petrol station).

Elemental God,
you who have flooded the earth with your rain,
rolled back a river, strolled on a sea
turned water to wine –
worked such great miracles of hydro-engineering,
will you not also meet our daily need,
lead your flock beside still waters,
allow us a cup of tea?

But I fear I am like my brother Israelite
who, in the hard times, the dry spells,
complained in the wilderness,
doubting the goodness of God.
I see countries stricken with drought;
I see peoples sick from dirty water;
I see villages swept away by floods
and I, too, ask, 'Is the Lord among us or not?'

forgetting, perhaps, that he is the supplier
of raw materials, a well-watered earth
with enough for all,

but a work in progress
requiring of us a restraint,
far-sightedness and love beyond our nature:
to know our need, then,
not just of H$_2$O, but living water . . .

But I fear I am also like the Samaritan woman
in her moral confusion,
prevaricating,
doubting the grace of God.
I see it is a long walk to the well;
I see it is impossible to stay clean;
I see the world puts a price on water;
and I, too, ask where such free living water can be found;

forgetting, perhaps, that Jesus himself
is an object lesson in grace:
essential elements
of God, gift-wrapped for us,
sent with the sole purpose
of saving us, faithless stewards
of his good earth and turning us into sons
born, not of man but of water and Spirit,
eau de vie,
your Spirit welling up in every heart that owns Christ,
a fountain of living water.

Living water!
Believers know
spiritual life could not have begun, could not go on
without you; know
that we ourselves, body, soul, spirit, are spiritually dead
without you; know
that you are free to all who ask, yet it is no small thing
to ask for such fiery spirit to course through our veins
designed, yes, to further our well-being
but soul-searing, this baptism
not with water but with fire, and the Holy Spirit:
curious element,

fire and water in one . . . two atoms of fire to one of water,
or vice versa?
(I can just imagine you looking over my shoulder, Lord,
as I scratch my head, smiling and thinking,
'Don't ask such daft questions!')

Earth, air, fire – and water,
essential elements.
Drink daily, and deep: and Lord, release your spring in me.

Optical Illusion

1 Samuel 16:1-13; John 9:1-41

You can't help feeling for the man born blind;
after all, surely anyone with half an eye
could *see* that he'd been healed,
see that he could see as well as you or I?

And you'd think they'd be pleased for him,
pleased for the light he could now see
and by which he could see, pleased that the light
of the world had broken in, set him free;

but no. All they could see, the Pharisees,
was the reversed image: white as black,
photographic negative, denying the miracle
and the miracle-worker, that quack

who, in order to fulfil its spirit,
set aside the letter of the law,
raised a few eyebrows, certainly, but opened eyes
which were ever blind before

and those who thought themselves clear-sighted
guides, perceptive and astute of mind
he left wondering if
against all odds, *they* were the blind . . .

Watch out, though: I have noticed
that, whenever we read of Pharisees
we pounce, quick to condemn:
Pharisaic as you please.

For all seeing, in the end, is partial
filtered through whichever lens obscures,
distorts our vision; one view becomes many,
as many as there are viewers;

Samuel and Jesse tempted, maybe,
to allocate their blessing
based only on outward appearance,
blinded by good looks and power dressing,

as are we. Pity the rock band
whose singer's voice is drop-dead gorgeous
but whose nose is sharp, whose chest is flat,
who, candidly, looks like the back of a bus;

perhaps I do not quite dare to say
that the fashion industry was spawned by the devil
but it's proved a much more effective tool
than the pitchfork in ruining the level

playing field, loading the dice
in favour of the brave and beautiful;
but God glances off the High Street image, urging us
to see through to his image in the soul.

And every age has its Pharisees,
lovers of the performance indicator,
target setting, league tables, statistics
and every kind of comparative data

which serve only to prevent us from seeing
the wood for the trees, burden, demoralise,
deflect our understanding, substitute
the cognoscenti for the wise:

having a certain knowledge, yes –
but lacking experience of what we know,
clanging cymbal, sounding brass
less of substance, more of outward show;

and so we Pharisees look through
our tick box lens, compounding our short sight;
so fraught with rules and regulations
we overlook the miracles of love and light.

And what of our rose-tinted specs?
Lens of false optimism, of illusion
that all is progress, and anything goes
because absolute truth's a delusion . . .

No, all seeing, in the end, is partial.
I do not see what you see:
though we stand shoulder to shoulder
the world will seem different to me

just as satellite imaging filters,
colours the landscape to show
now this, now that: vegetation, rock formation,
population – anything you need to know

in glorious swirls of abstract art
dazzling, puzzling, revealing, concealing,
providing so much information
hiding so much sense and feeling . . .

All seeing, in the end, is partial.
We are all born with a kind of blindness,
if only we could see it: see
that we are blind to kindness,

patience, goodness, love, joy, peace;
faithfulness, gentleness, self-control
fruits of the Spirit, character of Christ
radiance of immortal soul . . .

So let us look, Lord, to you: let us come
and sit close, and still, and let you look at us
and look, and look while your radiance rises
in us like the sun, rolls back the shadows

through which we peer darkly,
passing warped judgement, where we hide;
let the man born blind wait on the beach for you
shimmering light across incoming tide . . .

and not fear, not fear the flood of light
into my inmost being: yes, it will float
to the surface all that I've swept under
the carpet, and blind me to the mote

in my brother's eye until I've let you deal
with the plank in my own: good! So eat
your heart out, Canute! I long to feel
your ripples of light, Lord, round my feet:

pure, unfiltered light from creation's dawn
enabling me to see what you mean,
to see what you mean to me, new born
to see, even as I am seen.

Revival Meeting

Ezekiel 37:1-14; John 11:1-45

The church was dark, and cavernous;
I peered through the dimly-lit window let into the floor
and made out a medieval store:
bones, hundreds of bones set out neatly according to size
and separate, on a shelf above,
skulls tumbled together.
For a crazy moment,
I wondered if I should prophesy to the bones
and, if I did, whether the skull would find the bones that belonged to it
or whether I would end up with the wrong head
and two left feet.

I think maybe I did anyway.

More likely I'd be arrested and locked away
behind tall iron gates, with a sign
'Beware: mad dogs and Englishmen'.

But it *is* amazing what God can do with a bit of bone:
I mean, look at Eve!
And to think that everyone who has ever lived
will get up from their grave and stand before God –
yes, and those who have been cremated,
ashes to ashes, barely a fragment of bone remaining,
scattered to the four winds –
that would have been interesting, if Lazarus had been cremated:
but no problem, I'm sure, for God

who alone creates something from nothing
who alone breathes life.

And we're not speaking here of the skilled paramedic,
resuscitation on the way to hospital . . .
Israel's army was long dead, the bones dry;
and Lazarus four days in the grave:
Abraham, Isaac and Jacob breathe again,
for God is the God of the living, not of the dead.
This is the kiss of life with a difference;
more like re-creation.

Could there be hope, then, of revival
for that other fallen army:
that Church, that new house of Israel,
seeming so often no more lively than a pile of bones,
no more compelling than a decomposing corpse,
disjointed, bound, wistful, wasted?

What would it mean, for those bones to come together?
Movement:
no more rattling around in half-empty halls
but each to leave its pile of fellow bones
(sometimes he sent them out in twos)
and link to those who are different,
thigh bone to knee, to shin bone, to ankle,
to frivolous feet and tiresome toes
to grow, and find that they belong together . . .
old and young, trad and mod, high and low,
not critical, but complimentary,
complementary.

What would it mean, for there to be tendons linking?
Loyalty:
no more stubbornness and friction,
but a firm holding on to the truth of God,
flexible, elastic enough for us to differ in detail:
firm enough to keep out error and compromise,
keep us standing strong and fit for action.
This is a right binding,
allowing for give and take, but anchoring

the day's work, the night's dance, bound
and rebounding to the word of God:
held together.

What would it mean, for there to be flesh on the bones?
Love:
no more empty words, but an incarnation
a body expressing in word and deed
(and sometimes in what is left unsaid and undone)
always the highest good, be it of friend or foe.
For whilst the world doesn't know, doesn't care
what I believe, it may once again believe
when it sees how much I care,
when we recover our reputation:
'See how these Christians love
one another.'

What would it mean, to be covered with skin?
Calvary:
no more trusting our own 'best practice'
but each aware that, without the cross
and the shed blood of Christ
our wounds will not heal: we remain exposed
to the judgement of God, to enemy fire,
to knocking each other:
our only protection from him
whose robe of righteousness, torn
from his shoulders, is laid, like skin, on ours:
sealed for eternity.

Make us willing, Lord,
to go where you send us, to join, and grow
with those who are there; to know
what we believe and believe
what we know; to allow your Spirit
to show us how love should be lived,
and to know we are covered by Christ
for all eventualities.

May your Church walk again in the light, and *be* light:
not a final resting place for relics
but intensive care for new life . . .

Call us out, Lord, out of the dark cavern:
shout loudly!
Help us to remove one another's blindfolds,
untie one another's hands,
release one another's feet
and feel the blood rush into our numb fingers
and tingle
with all the excitement
of a new creation.

By Way of Betrayal

Matthew 21:1-11; Matthew 26:14–27:66

Why did he ask, Judas?
Why did he ask, 'Surely not I, Lord?'
He knew very well he was going to betray Jesus:
unless he didn't see it as betrayal.

Misunderstanding, frustration at his Lord's failure
to deliver: whatever.
The disciples' treasurer
sold their greatest asset down the river.

Just the first
of a long line of betrayals

Gethsemane.
Why did he ask the disciples to pray with him?
He might have known they would fall asleep
yet he had human need . . .

Three times he came and found them there,
those three whom he had awakened
to new life,
preferring sleep to prayer.
Betrayal.

And when at last
the time came – maybe they were blasé,
no one had been able to lay hands on him before –
the time of his arrest,

all of those with whom he had just shared bread,
all of them, all

who counted themselves so privileged
to be his closest followers, fled.
Betrayal.

So bring him to trial!
But on what grounds? Find a witness
who will quote his claim
to pull down, and rebuild the temple?

Quote, or misquote?
He never uttered such a threat: spoke rather
of himself. And such a charge, even if accepted,
would not secure the Roman vote

needed for execution, as Caiaphas well knew;
master of intrigue, wily fox
using and abusing
power for his own ends –

having failed to dish the dirt
on Jesus, puts him under oath,
against the law,
making the living God swear to his own hurt.
Betrayal.

Meanwhile, outside
Peter is also swearing;
as we do, so many of us
whenever we're put on the spot;

faced with accusation, he fumbles
for words, finds the wrong ones.
Flustered, fearful,
the one whom Jesus called the Rock, crumbles.
Betrayal.

From a man with a reputation
like Pontius Pilate
you wouldn't, of course, expect grace
(or that he'd take any notice of his wife)

so, failing to restore
his conscience alongside his career
he washes his hands; one man's weakness
undermines the strength of Roman law.
Betrayal.

From a Gentile,
understandable indifference;
from the Jewish priests and elders
uncomprehending enmity:

threading the crowd, sowing the seed,
incitement to religious hatred,
demanding a barbarian death
none would normally have agreed.
Betrayal.

And what is it about a crowd
that makes it so malleable,
so apt to park its mind,
become a loud mob?

So soon, to abandon the palm
and the shouts of 'Hosanna!'
So soon, to cry 'Crucify!'
to sing such a different psalm.
Betrayal.

Faced with the two,
Jesus of Nazareth and Jesus Barabbas:
what's in a name? Both fight for freedom
and both are 'sons of the father':

one is a common criminal,
commonly understood, fighting a common cause;
the other, an uncommon prophet
delighting, disturbing . . .

How is the crowd to be wise
as to which son, which father,
which freedom they'd rather have?
So one Jesus is saved, as his Saviour dies;

with well-deserved punishment waived
did Barabbas – do I? – find a different freedom?
One Jesus crucified on the other's cross
dying my death, and I am saved?

All this betrayal, then. Not so much tragic irony
as long-held plan?

I am Judas;
I am Peter; I am a sleepy disciple;
I am a false witness; I am priest and people;
I am the fickle crowd.

The very fact
that we cannot be trusted
to be courageous, loyal, wise, true
establishes the reason

for such a plan, and that its instrument
is treason:
therein lies its irony
its poetry, its grace.

Easter

And There Were Angels

John 20:1-18

A1 I remember, we were just sitting there, checking our 'to do' list –

A2 That's right: 1. 'Go down to earth' . . .

A1 Not something I usually look forward to; don't know what it is, lack of oxygen or something, but it always feels, sort of – oppressive.

A2 Mmm. Not the kind of day out we usually rush to sign up for. Bit different this time, though: even had to draw up a short list! This was the one we'd all been waiting for.

A1 And it was fair enough, Christmas OR Easter. Wouldn't have minded being in the host choir, though, and giving those shepherds the night of their lives! But we were privileged.

A2 2. 'Roll the stone away from the tomb'; well, that was no problem. I almost felt sorry for the guards; thought at first the shock had killed them, poor fellows; after all, they were only doing their duty. And I don't suppose for a minute their commanding officer believed a word they said. Angels, indeed! Maybe we should have worn mufti?

A1 3. 'Check everything is tidy'. You know, I hadn't quite realised he'd already be gone; of course, it's obvious when you think about it. It's not as if he needed us to drag him out and give him the kiss of life! Why, even down there they're beginning to talk about telekinesis and parapsychology –

A2 What?! Come on, no one actually saw it happen: even we don't know *how;* we just know God *did* raise Jesus from the dead.

A1 *We* do: but wasn't it incredible, how slow *they* all were to believe it? I mean, it's not as if he hadn't *told* them.

A2 But they're human. They're creatures of habit. They always think that if something hasn't happened before, or doesn't usually happen that way, it's impossible. And yet they say they believe in God! Some of them, at least. Whatever sort of a God?? Certainly not our glorious, all-powerful King. OK, I have to admit I don't always follow his thinking, but there's no doubting his infinite ability.

A1 But what on earth do they think happened if he didn't rise from the dead? If the Romans could have produced the body, they would – kept up their reputation, and scotched all those inconvenient rumours.

A2 I know, I know. And even if the disciples could have got past the guards and that hefty bit of rock, they'd hardly have been transformed into great missionary martyrs by what they knew to be a lie.

A1 And they saw him, for heaven's sake! Hundreds of them, after he rose from the dead.

A2 And Mary was the first – do you remember? Just as we were checking our list. I thought I'd heard someone crying – sobbing their heart out – and then she looked in and saw us.

A1 I never understood that. Why Mary, I mean: their women, so I understand, are notoriously emotional; the courts never trusted them as witnesses. But *he* trusted them! Perhaps they weren't so quick to try to explain it all away.

A2 Same at Christmas, wasn't it? Shepherds, I mean: the lowest of the low: why were they the first to be told? Perhaps for the same reason; they were prepared to go and see. Prepared to believe that there are more things in heaven and earth, Horatio . . .

A1 Raphael.

A2 You know what I mean – more than mere humans, or even angels, can get their minds around. Faith, not intellect, is the key; without faith, it's impossible to please God, or to know him.

A1 I still remember her face when she saw him. Her eyes still swollen and red from weeping, and then that look of utter amazement, incredulity, awe: and that brimming joy which would have known no bounds, had he not checked her – emotional, as ever – but with good reason! Not that she realised the implications, at the time; I don't think any of them did.

A2 Yet they sensed, even then, that it was not their hope but their dis-illusion that was misplaced; that this was not an end, but a begin-ning of something momentous which they would be called on to bring to birth; that although they did not understand the half, yet they were wholly committed, head over heels in love with their

Lord whom they could never again deny. They knew they were no longer the men and women they had been before: though they were not sure, yet, quite how they were different, quite how the whole world was different . . .

A1 What a morning!

A2 What a morning, for a world waking from a long night.

A1 What a morning, for heaven to welcome home its prince.

(Silence)

A2 Was there anything else on the list?

A1 Last one out, turn out the light.

An Open and Closed Affair

John 20:19-31

If you were part of our litigation-obsessed society, Thomas,
you'd probably sue
for defamation of character.

Doubting Thomas, we say,
meaning that died-in-the-wool sceptic
who has closed his mind,
closed the door
on the possibility of ever being convinced
about anything.

But that wasn't true
of you!
I believe
you were willing, open, *wanting* to believe
if only,
if only you could find a shred of real evidence.

But you weren't open to be taken for a ride –
another ride.
A ride on the back of a donkey into Jerusalem, to die with him,
yes, if that's how it had to be;
but not a ride into the land of make-believe,
a ride on the back of those other disciples, who tried to claim
the impossible, that a man who had died
was alive, and had walked through closed doors
to open up a whole new way of being:

I mean, come on fellas,
if it's true,
tell us how come you're all still sitting there, behind closed doors,
as though nothing's happened?

As a later doubting Thomas said
(one who had *not* closed his mind,
closed the door
on the possibility of being convinced
about anything,
but was willing, open, *wanting* to believe
if only,
if only he could find a shred of real evidence):
'These Christians will have to look a great deal more saved
    if I am to believe in their Saviour.'

That's what we need, we generations of doubting Thomases:
real evidence,
and an open door, through which we can come and find it.
(The risen Jesus may have been able to negotiate closed doors
but we who struggle to rise
can't.)

So where is it, this evidence?
Where are they, these open doors?
A church may boast that its doors are never locked during daylight
    hours
but often they are closed, and heavy
and what is glimpsed inside seems strange and uninviting;
either there is someone there
but my Thomas wants to be left alone;
or there is no one there
but he needs someone to draw him in.
The notice board tells him there is a family service
but his kids play football on Sundays, and then
they do the supermarket and the car-boot sale
and anyway, they wouldn't know the words, or the music
or how to be around God.

But through the week,
surely there are open doors?
At the office, the golf club, the pub –
wherever there's a Christian, surely *there*
is a life, an open book where a doubting Thomas may read about Christ,

see the hands of a disciple scarred in his service,
put his hand in the wounded side
pierced to make sure the disciple is truly dead
to self?
Is not every Christian an open door
to Christ?

If only!
If only we disciples
who *say* we believe in the risen Christ
who *say* we believe in the power of the Holy Spirit
would come out from behind those closed doors,
where we while away the time as though nothing has happened,
then perhaps the rest of the world could confront its doubts,
could see if it was true?

Or perhaps that's what we're afraid of.

But we must – surely we must!
Surely we must come out from behind those closed doors
of the gospel story
and be open to God,
open to be transformed into those
bold-speaking
earth-shaking
sold-out living
headline making
disciples whose Acts made it into Scripture, giving evidence,
real evidence
and an open door for the doubting Thomases of the day.

It's time we disciples came out,
declared ourselves
and trusted God to travel with us into the world outside.
No good saying that the doubting Thomases of *our* day should
pluck up the courage
to push that heavy, stiff and uninviting wood –
no, it's *we* who should pluck up the courage
to open those security doors:

not just so that 'they' can come in
but so that *we* can go out,
into the world where they are
and where God is
already at work
and get in on the act.

Thomas,
when you met Jesus for yourself
you were in no doubt
but confessed him Lord and God.

May we, today's disciples,
make space, and time, and an open door
for every doubting Thomas
to meet Jesus for himself:
up close and personal
Lord and God.

THIRD SUNDAY OF EASTER

Out of the Cool Box

Acts 2:14a, 36-41; Luke 24:13-35

Cool is cool.
Cool takes everything in its stride.
Cool is uncritical, unshockable.
Cool takes as cool finds.

Cool is cool.
Cool says, 'I'm OK, you're OK'.
Cool is up for it.
Cool says, whatever.

But I'm beginning to have my doubts about cool: it's a chilly fashion,
producing a pale, plasticine people.
Where is the fire, the conviction, the passion –
where is the heart?
Could it be that cool
is too cool for its own good?

Is it, in fact, dangerous
that enthusiasm is now perceived as dangerous?
That in such a complex, mine-filled, minefield of a world
the only safe course is to remain studiedly neutral?
That passion of any kind is seen as leading only to problems?
That fire in the belly is a folly, and a sickness to be cured?

But that is to deny
that lies and abuse and exploitation demand anger
and grief, and action, a naming and shaming of evil;
it is to deny
that splendour, and sacrificial living, and grace
should move us to awe, and to love, and to tears.

And we, we Christians,
do we do cool rather too well?
Anxious not to offend,
we suggest, keep to safe middle ground, defend,
and the preacher shakes hands at the end
as his flock files out, intact, unmoved, thinking of lunch.

Peter was another kettle of fish
who didn't do cool at all.
Anxious that no one should miss such great news
he warns, he pleads, he tells it straight
and then misses lunch, and supper too,
as his new flock, cut to the heart, queue at the narrow gate.

Sure, he wasn't deemed cool
by the high priests and the Roman rule;
his passion earned him abuse, ridicule
and prison walls; but three thousand lives
were turned around, three thousand hearts set free
to be fired by the flame of the Spirit.

What will it take, today,
to escape from the cool box?

The two on the road to Emmaus, they did it;
they escaped from the bleakness
of disappointment, confusion, suspected betrayal
because they had not sealed up their hearts
but were broken, open to be moved, warmed,
fired by words and bread of life

and they dropped everything, although it was late
– later now than when they urged him to stay –
and walked, ran, that seven miles back
back to Jerusalem, because the news could not wait,
the fire in their hearts burned
and darkness fell away.

Whereas we – we *ramble*,
our steps and our words unfocused,
stream of consciousness, better to travel
than to arrive, unwilling to accommodate
one with the temerity to think, or the passion to feel
he has an *answer*.

What will it take, today,
to escape from the cool box?

Is it, in fact, dangerous
that when we daren't admit to normal passion,
either the heart simmers and fumes and finally
boils over into violence
or, through dissembling and repression
atrophies?

If only Peter could come and preach next Sunday!
It's so long since we saw any souls saved . . .
But would we allow ourselves
to be cut to the heart,
or see only fundamentalist fervour
and flee, intact, unmoved?

If only Jesus could catch my train to work!
It's so long since I had a decent conversation . . .
But would I allow my heart, like Wesley's,
to be warmed into urgent life,
or hear only some chap with a bee in his bonnet
and change the subject back to football?

Unmoved, we are unmoving
and move no one.
If you, Lord Jesus,
said that lukewarm Christians made you sick,
I can't think you'd be any more impressed
by cool ones.

What will it take, today,
to escape from the cool box?
To rescue enthusiasm from the extremists?
To fan the flames of concern for the honour of God?
To install spiritual central heating in every church
running on burning truth, and radiant love and blazing grace?

You know what it will take, Lord;
dare I say
turn up the heat
melt us
fire us:

whatever.

Shepherd Songs

Acts 2:42-47; Psalm 23; 1 Peter 2:19-25; John 10:1-10

Bank Manager

The Lord is my celestial bank manager: I shall never go broke.
He makes me aware of the highest interest accounts;
he leads me to the best investments;
   he restores my credit-rating.
He guides me through all the small print
   because his reputation is at stake.

Even though I have reached the limit of my overdraft
   I will fear no bankruptcy
for you are with me:
   your warning letters and your personal adviser scheme,
     they comfort me.

You prepare a savings plan before me
   in the presence of my creditors.
You offer me all kinds of fringe benefits:
   I am rich beyond my wildest dreams!

Surely the unsearchable riches of Christ will provide for me
   all the days of my life,
and I will dwell in the extravagant grace of the celestial bank manager
   for ever.

Great Physician

The Lord is my great physician, I shall not lack healing.
He makes me take time for relaxation,
he leads me to programme rest into my schedule,
   he restores me, body and soul.

He guides me into fresh air and exercise:
    my divine fitness instructor.

Even though I go limping because of my aches and pains
    I will fear no breakdown,
for you are with me:
    your transplant surgery, your medicine, your strong Spirit, they
        comfort me.

You promise I am growing towards perfection;
    decay and death are a passing phase.
You show me my name tattooed on the palm of your hand:
    dare I believe I am that precious?

Surely your blood is flowing through my veins
    renewing my life,
and, one day made whole, I will dwell in the home of the great physician
    for ever.

Nerd's 23rd

The Lord is my worldwide webmaster; I shall not search in vain.
He makes me browse the delights of richly colourful, sustaining sites;
he leads me to pages of virtual peace and tranquillity;
    he refreshes my screen.
He leads me in pathways that are true;
    his URL is always to be found.

Even though I surf through error messages flagging that final crash
    I will fear no virus
for you are with me;
    your scandisk and your help screen they comfort me.

You prepare a network before me
    in the presence of the hackers.
You power me to devise a search engine bearing my name;
    my head is spinning: I have run out of RAM!

Surely your saving and your ultimate back-up disk will provide for me
    all the days of my life,
and I shall dwell in the domain of the worldwide webmaster
    for ever.

Line Manager

The Lord is my line manager, I shall not be exploited.
He makes me part of a well-resourced team,
he leads me to take time to reflect, take stock,
    he restores my work-life balance.
He guides me to speak and act with integrity
    because I am known as one of his team.

Even though I live in the shadow of challenging targets
    I will fear no pressures,
for you are with me:
    your appraisals, and your prayers, and your praise, they comfort me.

You will defend me against all the unreasonable demands
    and accusations of other bosses.
You even reward me for a job well done;
    such employers must be few and far between!

Surely job satisfaction and promotion prospects are there for me
    all the days of my life,
and I will dwell in the security of my manager's pension plan
    for ever.

Refugee

Psalm 31:1-5, 15, 16; 1 Peter 2:2-10; John 14:1-14

Can you imagine what it's like, to look down and make out a world
criss-crossed with long, spidery lines of people walking,
stumbling, picking themselves up, hoisting children, doggedly
    marching on;
or running, desperately looking for valley, scrub or stones to hide them,

refugees

from flood, fire, earthquake and famine,
from all manner of killing and persecution and ethnic cleansing?
Tens of thousands in Sri Lanka,
a hundred thousand in Lebanon,
two and a half million in Sudan alone,
twenty million or so, of one kind or another, the world over
and that's just those who reached the United Nations Commission's in-tray
or today's news.

Can you imagine what it's like, to know that the door is shut behind you,
the enemy is snapping at your heels and there is no way back?
No bad dream, this, but a waking nightmare with little prospect of a
    new dawn.
Can you imagine what it's like, to be so utterly uprooted, to be
    just you
no familiar fields or hills,
no sound of nearby river or mail truck on the dirt road
no tradition, no story, no more birds singing in the tree by your door
no door
no home
no belongings
no belonging

just you
silhouette torn from your photo frame,

you, and so many other silhouettes, stumbling, walking, running away
because the world, which had seemed fair enough, on the whole,
has suddenly shown its savage face: civilisation slips, is stripped away
and it's just you,
taken by surprise, shocked, stumbling

stumbling away.
Refugees are those who flee what lies behind
and we are duly appalled at the terrors that put them to flight
forgetting, perhaps
that refugees are also those who seek a refuge ahead,
a refuge, surely, that must in the end be more than a makeshift encampment,
a sprawling junk sculpture resourced or under-resourced
by overworked aid agencies;
provision, yes – of a kind,
but provisional, surely?

Such is our world that always, it seems, there has been need for refuge:
from the days of the cities of refuge for those who had unintentionally
    shed blood,
rescuing them from too rough justice;
from the days of altar and sanctuary offering, if you could reach them,
    asylum
(though many since Thomas a Beckett have found such a system –
    unsatisfactory)

refugees,
so many fleeing
so many evils in the world; finding
so little refuge

we look at our TV screens and shake our heads at the seeming indifference
    of God,
at man's inhumanity to man, and maybe reach for our chequebook:
at least we can contribute to some kind of provisional solution . . .

refugees,
so many fleeing
so many evils in ourselves; finding
so little refuge

and do we look at our TV screens and shake our heads at the so-called
 reality
that markets godlessness beneath a mask of normality
and weep for all of us who are seduced by what is no kind of solution?

Looking down again at those long, spidery lines of people criss-crossing
 the world:
do we not see ourselves
now walking, now stumbling, now running, now hiding
from evils that beckon or threaten outside of ourselves,
and from their insistent echo within?

And it's right that we run from evil: but not headlong, not blindly
or how do we know we'll not end up escaping the lion only to meet the
 bear?

For in all this world of refugees
there is no lasting refuge;
and perhaps we should not be surprised, shocked –
for we are, after all, strangers and pilgrims, passing through
and everything is provisional. One evil follows another and, what is
 more, we
who look for refuge are both refugee and enemy.

And yet there *is* a place, places, of refuge
even now being prepared, just with you and me in mind: a new dawn!
Nothing makeshift or provisional about this master plan;
and there will be a homecoming, such a homecoming
that will rewrite our whole understanding of 'home'

and there *is* a person, the Lord our refuge,
a person of this world, yet not of this world!
He will lift us when we stumble, walk with us, run with us
hold us, shelter us, yes, carry us even –
as we criss-cross this world on our way, aware or not, to the next . . .

Dare to believe, and trust: only trust . . .
for it is the One who shared our homelessness
who guarantees us home.

Tourist Information

Acts 17:22-31; 1 Peter 3:13-22

Weekend city breaks:
where would you stay?
Paris, Barcelona,
Venice, Prague?
Culture vultures are spoilt today for choice.

But then – no question;
Athens dazzled the world
with the splendour of her famous sons
architects, philosophers,
statesmen and poets,
buzzing with ideas,
polishing their wit and wisdom,
furnishing their city with glory, and a guaranteed
tourist trade.

And the visitors are impressed, and stop and stare
and point, and point their cameras,
their camcorders and hope that, three weeks from now,
they'll remember which temple, which square,
which city even.

And Paul, first-century-tourist – was he impressed? Yes,
surely: not being a Philistine.
But Paul, the missionary-tourist sees differently:
is arrested, this time, not by the beauty
(nor yet by the authorities)
but by the dishonour that would undermine
his God . . .

It was said that in Athens
it was easier to find a god than a man,
the city being awash with idols,
pretty silver, glitzy gold
gritty stone:
hand-made, brand-made
man-made
tidal waves of idols.

And Paul is impressed by the want of the wealthy city
    by the illusion of its wisdom
    by the Babel of its fine buildings
    by the presence of gods, and by the scandalous absence of God.

Impressed?
Distressed, jealous,
gutted that the glory of God is given to others:
and goaded to action.

And me?
Oh, I just go to see the sights.
And do I *see*?
Or do I just play with my new digital camera?

I have a picture of the brave new glass-and-steel shopping mall
but I did not *see* the breaking of the tenth commandment,
pity the poor
feel the righteous anger of God
or pick up my pen.

What sort of tourist am I?
A twenty-first century, consumerist creature
who travels only to taste, to test the water, take a titbit or two, and
    move on.
I am passive, pale, provoked by nothing
except the price of petrol and parking.
I do not see that the world is dying of consumption,
that its prince is laughing

while God is crying out to be heard,
to have his honour restored
through me.

I have a picture of the late-night West End show
but I did not *see* the breaking of the seventh commandment,
pity the prostituted
feel the righteous anger of God
or walk out.

What sort of tourist am I?
A twenty-first century, promiscuous creature
who travels only to flirt with the world, to steal a kiss, escape and play
    the field.
I am seduced, supine, stirred by nothing
except the salacious.
I do not see that the world is dying of debauchery,
that its prince is laughing
while God is crying out to be heard,
to have his honour restored
through me.

I have a picture of the temple treasures
but I did not *see* the breaking of the second commandment,
pity the deceived people
feel the righteous anger of God
or tell the truth.

What sort of tourist am I?
A twenty-first century, idolatrous creature
who travels only to worship the sun, the surf, the self who surely
    deserves it . . .
I am fickle, profligate with my favours, fired by nothing
except the fear of fastening my colours to the mast.
I do not see that the world is dying of faithlessness,
that its prince is laughing
while God is crying out to be heard,
to have his honour restored
through me.

Tourist information –
about what is,
or what is lacking?
about what is,
or what should be?
Am I here simply to see
or to *see* – with the eyes of my heart enlightened?

I have picked up the leaflets directing me to the sights;
they give me information,
they tell me where – but not why;
a table of contents, but no story.
But what good is seeing,
if it does not lead to illumination,
if it does not lead to believing?

What sort of tourist am I? Please,
a twenty-first century missionary-tourist
who travels also to understand the signs of the times and the place;
who seeks to make uncommon sense, to speak the truth, incensed
by the celebration of all except the one true God;
who sees that the world is dying without Christ,
that the prince of this world is defeated
while God is crying out to be heard,
to have his honour restored
through me

and I say,
'Here I am, Lord: send me.'

Foundlings

Daniel 7:9-14; Ephesians 1:15-23

Perhaps it's the ultimate tale,
better even than a simple 'rags to riches':
the tale of the foundling,
mystery child deposited on a poor man's doorstep
theirs and yet not theirs,
family yet ever a stranger
as he makes his way through life
surprising them with a resourcefulness, a wit, a wisdom
certainly not acquired from them;
following a star they can't discern
straight on, taking the consequence . . .

And where will it end?
It is so important, to know where it will end,
to know that he *will* find his destiny,
his true identity,
that he *will* arrive home,
the baby hidden when his royal parents fled,
found by the ancient woodcutter, left at that humble door;
he is the lost prince
restored now to his rightful throne.

It would hardly be the ultimate tale
if he were simply to live and die
a poor man's child, however laudable
their simple lives.

It's as if we all have something of the foundling in us,
an echo, as it were,
from the foundation of the world
insisting that we, too, were destined

for higher things: that we too were left
on the wrong doorstep . . .

And they know, the TV programme planners;
they know, and pander to our fantasies
and we sign on, willingly,
not just for the chance of fifteen minutes' fame
but on the off chance that we will be *found,*
that the world will recognise
we too were left on the wrong doorstep
and restore us,
princes and princesses,
to our rightful kingdom;

and no amount of evidence,
or experience – nothing, it seems –
will shake our eternal optimism.

Thus did a nation mourn Diana,
grief at a royal tragedy compounded
by desolation
that the myth of the fairytale princess
was cruelly exposed,
hope of a happy ending, not just for her
but for us
crashed.

And was it not his story too? Jesus,
the foundling.
Deposited not on the doorstep but,
from who knows where
in Mary's womb; from the very beginning
prompting the world to ask,
'Who is he?'
Growing up in the family,
but not of it: son, and stranger
following a strange star
which charts his course from carpenter's bench
to Calvary's cross
and from height of heaven
to depths of hell –

and where will it end?
It is so important to know where it will end,
to know that he *will* find his destiny,
his true identity,
that he *will* arrive home;
the baby in whom dwelt all the fullness of God,
found in human form in a moment of time;
he is the Saviour of the world
restored now to his rightful throne.

It would hardly be the ultimate tale
if he were simply to live and die
a wandering Jewish chippy, however laudable
his life and teaching.

But we do know the end
or at least, the beginning of the end:
that the foundling is back with his rightful father,
quest completed, foe defeated
come of age now,
come into his inheritance – ascended,
however that may be,
and the whole world at his feet.

But what is that to us,
who have some echo of the foundling in us, too?
Bully for him,
and all those other fairytale princes –
but what of Diana? And what of us?

Oh, don't you see?
This, this is the tale which, from the foundation of the world
echoes in our souls,
insisting that we, too, *are* destined
for higher things;
which sowed that seed of hope and expectation
of a happy ending

for we were indeed born
to be princes, princesses,
children of a heavenly King:
who, through our own fault, found ourselves
bundled out of Eden and left
on the doorsteps of the world until such time
as we were found again,
found by the one who, himself, became a foundling
for us,

declaring, by his own rising
and homecoming to heaven
that death does not draw a line under our destiny:
our true identity
emerges after, happily
ever after
when we are restored
by, and to our father in heaven.

Insufferable

1 Peter 4:12-14, 5:6-11

I used to be even more mystified
about suffering
when I thought the Bible was telling me
to rejoice in it:
but that would surely be
insufferable.

Suffering
is,
because that's the way the world is,
so volcanoes erupt, and lightning strikes.
Suffering
is,
because I foul things up,
so relationships fail, and disease spreads.
To rejoice in such suffering
would be to take leave of my senses,
to stifle my heart and my conscience,
add insult to injury:
insufferable.

Suffering
is, too,
because of the darkness
which cannot stand the light
and lashes out at the first sight
of the sun rising,
of the Son of God rising,
of the body of Christ rising,
surprising the world
in its guilty slumber

with an unwelcome alarm call;
crash! And again,
body clock slammed into silence
and a thousand voices
cry out in pain:
insufferable

inevitable
if we walk in the light,
as he is in the light,
we will find ourselves caught in the crossfire
of all the fiery darts of the devil.
But at least we know we're on the right path,
the same path as our saviour:
there is our case, our cause for rejoicing.

But I am still mystified
about suffering
when I think that mine consists
in forgoing Sunday shopping,
waiting for the subject to be changed when I mention church,
being unable to share my children's world view:
and so I am treated with mild caution,
a tad marginalised
because I am a little mad
(though not dangerous)
and I fret because I do not feel at home
in my comfort zone.

And then I read of the suffering
of your servants
who cannot work because they are sent to the back of the queue
who cannot learn because it is forbidden
who cannot eat because they cannot earn
who cannot sleep because there is no room in the cell to lie down
who cannot dream because their torn backs scream aloud
who cannot speak because walls have ears
who cannot live for tomorrow because it may never come
who cannot die today, because their time has not yet come

and I find it
insufferable
to speak of us both in the same breath
and I wonder
what they are doing wrong
to deserve such suffering,
daily to face death?

And then I think, no, NO!
What are they doing *right*,
to be *trusted* with such suffering?

And I – would I have the grace
to love my Lord to the end,
or would I collapse at the first sight of blood,
not fit for the race?
Is that why I suffer only snide remarks
while others are shot?

And I am still mystified
about suffering
that I, who suffer less, know less
of the joy of the Lord;
that they, who suffer more, know more
of the Spirit of the Lord
and in their cells there is an echo of praise
and in my church there is just an echo.

Perhaps this too is a kind of suffering:
not to know the tangible presence of Christ
transforming my terror;
not to hear the clear voice of the Spirit
loving me into total trust;
not to glimpse the transcendent glory of God
beckoning me;
that, that indeed, would be cause for rejoicing,
could even make me feel,
perhaps,
that no suffering was too great a price to pay

for such grace?
Is it only in deep darkness
that such a bright light can shine?
Do the nightmares of earth's night fade
when I have one foot in heaven?

Or is that the insufferable arrogance
of a comfortable ignorance?
Grace, after all, is free . . .

So I am still mystified
about suffering
but that is no excuse for distraction:
I must anchor my speculation
in prayer for discernment
of my own subtle suffering
and my response . . .

The enemy, after all, is the same
whether he comes with AK47
or silk cushions:
insufferable.

A Question of Spin

Acts 2:1-21; 1 Corinthians 12:3b-13

Take a word – any word –
and, with a little influence in the right places,
spin it into something
completely different.

Wicked. Grass. Gay. Cool.

Take two words – any two words –
mix with a little negative history, plenty of ridicule,
a dash of irony, and there they go:
for ever devalued.

Little innocents. Character property. *Holy Spirit.*

To most of us, it sounds more like a threat
than the gracious promise of God
because we don't do 'spirit' very well in the West
and 'holy' has us racing for shelter –

doesn't it? What visions does 'holy' conjure up for you?

Plaster saints (real or manufactured),
brittle, bright, full of silent reproof;
shining, white, light: untouchable –
wipe your shoes and keep off the grass (both sorts);
pious, sanctimonious, full of high-sounding words
echoing against hollow lives;
virtuous, unsullied – but with the virtue born
of never having had to resist temptation;
superiority of moral fibre –
imagined or, worse, real;

someone whose good deeds are enough
to put you off the whole idea of charity;
who has reached such pinnacles of virtue
that they can only look down on the rest of the human race:
holier than thou
holy terrors.

'Holy' has to be a word in need of a make-over.

Perhaps we should think rather of 'holistic',
dealing positively with the whole of who I am;
integration of fragmented being,
knowing me as a person, not a number;
or think 'whole', as in good wholemeal bread
and all the goodness of whole foods;
or 'whole-hearted' as in welcome
or in the commitment of bride and groom;
think 'wholesome' entertainment,
refusal of smut, soft porn, violence;
'whole blood', 'whole milk', undoctored
offering all their natural goodness to build strength;
this, these are more like the Holy Spirit of God:
whole spirit of God, on a mission to make us
hale and hearty
whole people.

And 'spirit', let's face it, has an equally bad press.

Spirits? Ghosts, unconvincing in white sheets
or, more convincing, in ectoplasm;
spooky tales, the stuff of children's fantasy,
or Hammer Horror movies;
mediums at psychic fairs, bringing forbidden,
fraudulent 'comfort' to the bereaved;
or something rather airy-fairy
fêted by wearers of long earth-coloured skirts and green chiffon;
something not of this world.
Risky: rather keep my feet on the ground;

supernatural: some even talk of witchcraft, evil spirits;
dodgy territory: steer well clear.
And all those strange words marshalled under 'spiritual':
transcendental, numinous, ineffable
mystical . . .
Incomprehensible.

Can we still rescue this 'spirit' from ruin?

I talked to the man whose elderly wife had died:
'She was full of spirit, right to the end,' he said proudly;
and to the mum whose toddler was into everything:
'Real spirit of adventure, he's got,' she enthused.
Which of us would not want to be in good spirits?
For one who is lacking in spirit
depresses himself and his neighbour
and is only half alive.
And which of us would not covet that spirit of peaceful resistance
of Ghandi or Luther King;
the courage of Daniel, the patience of Job,
the spirit of power, and love, and a sound mind?
Which of us would not covet the spirit of Christ-likeness
of Jesus Christ? Well now, that is exactly
what is on offer:
the Holy Spirit of Christ.

It's time we wised up,
to how words have been spun;
how 'unearthly' which promised a glimpse of heaven
now denotes an unearthly row;
how 'immaterial' used to be something not restricted by matter
but now means something which does not matter.
Perhaps we need to lay these verbal ghosts,
redeem our words
before they rob us of reason, and cheat us
of our rightful inheritance:

come, Holy Spirit.

Ordinary Time

Let's Say the Grace Together

2 Corinthians 13:11-13; Matthew 28:16-20

The grace of the Lord Jesus Christ, the love of God, and the fellowship of the Holy Spirit be with us all.   *2 Corinthians 13:13*

I mean,
how else to end the prayer meeting?
And if we're feeling a bit modern, a bit daring,
why, we'll look up, look at each other,
maybe even – smile?
Though there'll always be some
who will keep their head bowed
out of reverence, from embarrassment,
or for fear they'll forget the words.

It's almost too easy, though:
a formula
like 'Yours sincerely' at the end of the letter,
however insincerely meant;
too easy to speak too lightly
those weightiest of words:
grace – love – fellowship
to toss them off as some kind of pleasant postscript
instead of the very stuff of our life's work.

And what is this – the Son coming before the Father?

Yes, because grace is first: always first.
How else, apart from Christ,
how else would we ever know
that our God was like this:
a God of love –
such love?

Christ has our shape – though it was not always so;
Christ has our stature – though inside is greater than out;
Christ has our speech – though pregnant with new sense;
Christ has our sorrow – not only face to face, then, but heart to heart.

Jesus we see, cutting and planing wood;
Jesus we hear, calling his brothers to eat;
Jesus we know, in the sharing of wine at sunset;
Jesus is one of us: tradesman, one of the family, friend.

And it's only little by little,
when we see the storm stilled, and cannot believe our eyes;
when we hear him challenge the chief priests,
and cannot believe our ears
that we ask, do we *really* know this man?
Is he *really* one of us, or could he be –
Christ?

But there is more,
shockingly more –
a shock that rocks our very world to its core:
this man,
this carpenter's mate
this fisherman's friend
turned teacher, preacher, healer
turns out to be Christ, yes,
God's anointed, Messiah

but where is the proud warrior?
Where is the pomp and ceremony,
where the panache, the plaudits, the victory parade?

This Messiah
chooses the shockingly inefficient method of saving
not just the nation, but the world
not just for now, but for ever
not all together, but *one by one;*
not by might, nor by power
lest any should later sue for harassment

but by being, himself
the heart-warming, heart-rending embodiment
of the grace
which is God bending low
to lift me up.

The grace of our Lord Jesus Christ
is, then, none other than the love of God
transposed into a human key and played,
played out in life and, shockingly, in death.

Yes, because grace is first: always first.
How else, apart from Christ,
how else would we ever know
that our God was like this:
a God of love –
such love?

What is man, that you are mindful of him?
That you even remembered those tiny specks of dust
you once told to multiply
on that miniscule planet:
let alone ached for them, wept for them,
wrestled with them, laid your very life on the line
to restore in them that full humanity
that mirrors your divinity?
Couldn't you have just scrubbed that lot
and brought out a new version?

But you are not into built-in obsolescence
but into love, which never gives up
as long as there is the slightest chance
that we might lay our heady freedom at your feet;
the wounded feet
of love bending low
in order to lift up.

And we are the lowly company of those
who have been lifted up

and set alight by the Holy Spirit, who takes
the grace of Christ and works it into our being; who takes
the love of God and works it into our doing
so that we,
divided by culture and class,
generation and gender, talent and taste
become one
before you:
   loved by the same Father
   lifted by the same Son
   linked by the same Spirit . . .

If only.

If only we would realise,
as we say the grace together,
that it's down to us now:
God has done his bit.
Grace, love, fellowship
are ours for the asking –
as much
or as little
as we want.

Mind the Gap

Deuteronomy 11:18-21, 26-28; Matthew 7: 21-29

The first thing you should do when you go to someone's house
     for the first time
is examine their fridge magnets.
At least that'll tell you what they *want* you to think about them.
Though of course, there may be a bit of a gap between the fridge
and the reality of the kitchen sink.

It's so *easy* to beg, borrow or steal someone else's words today; it's pretty
     well become an art form.
Several art forms, in fact: not only fridge magnets but
T-shirts, tattoos, stencils, stickers, everything you need to customise
     your car,
rucksack, pencil case, desktop – write it large,
otherwise they won't know who you are:
neither will you
and change it often,
otherwise they'll think you haven't got a life:
and maybe you'd begin to doubt it too.

It's so *easy* to borrow words: because words are everywhere.
I dread to think how many are fogging up the ether, blog upon blog,
like so many messages in bottles launched by the shipwrecked
in the vain hope that someone, somewhere, will intercept and rescue
     them from nonentity.
Though of course, there may be a bit of a gap between the spin
and the reality of life that left them with nothing better to do than blog.

It worries me a bit that Jesus is the *Word* of God
because we can treat his words in the same cavalier fashion as any other:

as a vehicle for an ego trip
as a cover for hollowness
as a declaration of an intent we have no intention of following through
instead of receiving him as the word *made flesh*.

We read that no one can say 'Jesus is Lord' except by the Holy Spirit.
Oh, but we can – depending on what you mean by 'say';
anyone can articulate the words: but only in a manner of speaking:
'Lord! Lord!' we say, maybe daily
but is it a humble, willing submitting of spirit to Spirit, reporting for duty
  of serving soldier,
or a plea for attention, for action, for acceptance by association
with those who seem to have something going for them,
even the Lord himself?

For of course, there may be a bit of a gap between my spoken word
and the reality of the life that gives the lie to its integrity.

So many words
so easy to be word perfect
and for the words to be perfectly empty.

Even as I write, I long that people would stop writing
stop wrapping the simple truth around with layers of qualification
explanation, justification, modification, rationalisation: obfuscation . . .
Perhaps we should all limit ourselves to just those words which will lodge
in our hearts and minds, just those words which will fit
on our hands, our foreheads, our doorposts
our fridge magnets

and do them

and that would be enough
and only that would be enough
to bridge the gap between head and heart,
between mouth and money
and avoid judgement.

Easier said than done,
with such a mountain of unspoken excuses between word and deed:
accommodation
(so many of these -ation words seem to be less-than-helpful man-made
    prevarication.)
But, if not lived out, fleshed out, with every repetition words are weakened
wear thin, like old clothes doing the rounds of the charity shops
and we are left in threadbare coats, once good, but which impress no
    one now
and barely keep out the cold.

Moses might have found a use for fridge magnets:
'Hear O Israel, the Lord is our God, the Lord alone,
and you shall love the Lord your God with all your heart',
and maybe a series with the ten tommandments,
and given a set to each of the children of Israel . . .

But now?
Yes, we still need reminders more than we need to be taught new
    things;
but now God wants to write his words FIRST
on our hearts
only *then* on paper, plastic or web page;
now God wants to invite the world to read FIRST
our lives poured out
only *then* our outpourings.

Of course, there will always be a bit of a gap between who I am
and who, I trust, Jesus is making me: just a *bit*?!
and any words must be carefully spoken, written,
(for I shall have to give account of each careless one):
words that do not limit Christ
to what can be seen in me
but neither presume
experience which is not yet mine.
I do mind that gap
between what I want people to think about me
and the reality of what I am; I mind it dreadfully.

God, I guess, will mind it even more:
and, two minds being better than one
we will work together
to bring together
the now and then, present and future perfect
Lordship of Christ.

I Can Fit You In

Psalm 50:7-15; Matthew 9:9-13, 18-26

'He can fit you in on Thursday week at 5.20.'
'I should just have time in between aerobics and picking up the children.'
'They can grab a sandwich on the way out to football.'
'We'll give you a ring if there's a cancellation.'

Twenty-first century living
resembles nothing so much as one of those Chinese puzzles:
once you take it out of the box, there's absolutely NO WAY
you can juggle those pieces to get them all back in
and it's obvious that there are far too many,
someone must have slipped in a few extra when you weren't looking

just like your diary

and so they issue directives about work-life balance
and charts to analyse how you spend an average 24 hours
making sure you allocate time for work and play,
sleep, family, food and exercise – oh, and filling in charts.

And for those of us of a religious persuasion,
there's an extra bit to squeeze in, whenever we can manage it,
around 10 till 11 on a Sunday morning (and for a few minutes
every morning, if we're *really* religious): the God slot,

as the BBC would call it, in a magnanimous gesture
to the religious right, and the religious right passes on the favour to God.

Heaven help us when God is timetabled into our lives
like a token RE lesson: first to go when the pressure's on.

God slot, God of the gaps, God channel – God forgive us!
As if you didn't cover all the slots, fill all the gaps, invade all the channels.

The effrontery, of trying to fit you into our lives, somewhere, somehow
when in you we live, and move, and have our very being;
of thinking that a nod in your direction will insure us
(should the atheists be wrong) against all things that go bump in the night,
register us on some divine database,
gain for us a toehold on eternity . . .

Yet all is not lost,
for you do not refuse our first, faltering steps;

yet all is lost,
for you seek the love that we don't yet have, so cannot give.

'It's not that I'm not pleased to see you on Sunday: truly, I am.
But it breaks my heart to know it was duty, fear even,
that brought you, the 'ought' of your childhood:
you do not yet know how much I love you . . .

'It's not that my heart doesn't leap when you call my name
in the morning; but why do you leave me a voicemail,
send me an email, when I long for a leisurely conversation?
I love you: can you not love me a little?

'It's not that I don't appreciate that time on the air;
songs of praise are always music to my ears;
but if only *every* word spoken, *every* picture screened
were true, honourable, just, pure and worthy of praise.'

Why have we chopped our lives into little pieces?

Is it the fault of Henry Ford's production line?
It's more *economic* if one shapes and another welds;
if one makes nails and another hammers them;
if one cuts and another sews; but . . .

but it's like the six men who planted potatoes, day in, day out;
day in, day out: they sang, and planted in time with the music;
then one day along came the engineer who designed a machine
so that only two men were needed: progress!

But there was no more singing.

Like Humpty Dumpty, we've all of us had a great fall.
We've got egg on our face, and the pieces of shell
lie scattered; no amount of king's horses or king's men
can fit those pieces back together, integrate our lives again.
Who, then?

Only the King himself . . .

if, once again we could see him as all in all:
the source of every workman's skill
the divine spark of fun that engenders play
the shepherd in whose safe-keeping we sleep
the love that bonds fragmented lives into families
the generous giver of earth, rain, sun, seed and harvest
the strength of our bodies that live, move
and have their very being in him!

Pull me together, Lord.
Let the threads of your love pull all the parts of my life together
and hold me close;
I cannot fit you in – you are not part of my life:
by your grace,
I, every part of me,
am part of yours.

Unsuccessful Interview

Romans 5:1-8; Matthew 9:35-10:8, (9-23)

Interviewer Paul – thank you for agreeing to be interviewed; I thought we'd never catch up with you!

Paul My pleasure; I'm always happy to talk to anyone who'll listen!

Interviewer Here we go, then. What is your idea of perfect happiness?

Paul To see someone realise the truth – that they can be at peace with God.

Interviewer Er, I'll put *'world peace'* –

Paul You will not! That's not what I said – there will never be world peace, because there will always be those who turn their back on God; suffering is inevitable. But people can be forgiven, set free, know the love of God in Jesus Christ.

Interviewer (*To himself:* Now I know why they wished me luck. Trust me to get a religious nutter.) OK. What is your greatest fear? Snakes and scorpions are popular . . .

Paul Fear? What kind? I fear God: because he is holy, and not to be trifled with; and yet, I don't fear him, because he loves me: so much, that he sent his Son to die for me, when I least deserved it. As for the rest – snakes, scorpions, no! God has protected me from those, and will protect me from everything that would prevent me doing what he asks of me.

Interviewer . . . *fatalistic*. What will be, will be, eh? And what do you most deplore in yourself? (*Aside:* Don't tempt me!)

Paul Impatience – with delays; restlessness – until everyone knows about Jesus. Maybe getting carried away with my own enthusiasm and going on a bit.

Interviewer ... *going on a bit.* OK. What is your greatest extravagance? Not that you seem the indulgent sort, unfortunately for our readers.

Paul Foreign travel, I guess. How else will people get to hear the good news?

Interviewer Ah, *travel.* And what objects do you always carry with you?

Paul The tools of my trade: tent-making – I prefer to earn my living, not be a burden to anyone. And the tools of my other trade: the scriptures, pen and paper; I'm a great letter-writer, you know.

Interviewer I know ... and for luck, rings, say, rabbit's foot?

Paul *Luck? Rabbit's foot??* It didn't do much for the rabbit. And what's *luck*, in an ordered universe?

Interviewer OK, OK, I shouldn't have asked. Now – what keeps you awake at night?

Paul Lots of things: storms at sea; late-night preaching; prison chains interfering with my singing, followed by earth-quakes; oh, and the occasional vision.

Interviewer ... *bad dreams* ...

Paul No, no! Not dreams, and certainly not bad; glimpses of heaven, such that even I have to say that words fail me ...

Interviewer As if this interview wasn't already too serious to print, but I have to ask the question: for what cause would you die? Your family, perhaps?

Paul I would die, if by my death any other life could be saved – not just for now, but for eternity. Of course, it is Jesus' death that wins for us life with God for ever: but if my death could help anyone understand that, and receive him ... To die, with the prospect of being with God, is not loss, you know, but gain.

Interviewer ... *saving life* ... *one with universal force* ... I wonder, could we lighten up a bit? This is the Sunday supplement, you know. Can I ask how you'd like to be remembered? Most dramatic conversion, most crossings of the Mediterranean, most jail-breaks?

Paul	I don't think I care much about being remembered; I'll be living, you know, and not just in people's memories! And I'm not in this for the knight-hood or the history books; I can't help but do what I'm doing: that's what being bowled over by Jesus does for you. Perhaps – just as some-one's father in Christ: that would be – heart warming.
Interviewer	. . . *father figure*. OK; finally – What's the most important lesson life has taught you? Remember, I only have a few column inches, and a draconian editor . . .
Paul	Forgive me for saying so, but that's a singularly ill-phrased question: does nobody study logic and dialectic any more? Life, my friend, teaches us nothing. Life is neutral: a kalei-doscope of people, places and events: what we learn from them depends on who or what we choose to listen to. First, I listened to the Jewish rabbis: they taught me that the Lord God is one, and holy and I am to love him with all my heart, soul, mind and strength.
Interviewer	*(Sighs)* First. There's more?
Paul	There certainly is. Second, I listened to Jesus who taught me that was impossible: however hard I tried to rule my out-ward actions, my heart was not right. But then – the greatest lesson of all – he taught me that, like Abraham, I can be justi-fied before God by faith: by faith in Jesus himself, his death on the cross, his rising from the dead and his presence in me, in the person of his Holy Spirit, to transform my life.
Interviewer	Hold on! I'll have to edit that, I'm afraid – it does sound a bit preachy, and we have to be careful not to offend, you know.
Paul	Oh, no you don't! The reason your church is so feeble these days – if you'll pardon my saying so – is that people have only had your carefully edited version of the good news. Take God out of the good news, and you're left with zero news: no news worth listening to; that's not being sensi-tive, that's short-changing people in need and dishonour-ing God.
Interviewer	*(To himself:* Why wasn't I on last week? That nice guy who just said 'Whatever . . .' But this Paul! Admirable, I'm sure, in his way: but seriously unprintable . . .)

Quote Unquote

Matthew 10:24-39

There are so many things that Jesus *didn't* say
that we might wish he had
like 'Come to me, and all your problems will be solved!'
'Go on, spoil yourself: because you're worth it!'
'Follow me, and I will make you healthy, wealthy and wise!'
'Look after yourself! Good luck! Take care!'

Shucks.

And there are so many things that Jesus *did* say
that we might wish he hadn't
like 'I have not come to bring peace, but a sword!'
  'If they persecuted me, they will persecute you!'
  'If you love your family more than me, you're not worthy of me!'
  'Deny yourself! Take up your cross! Follow me!'

Shucks.

How often do we quote God's care for the sparrow
and the fact that we are worth more . . .
But Jesus does not say that therefore sparrows will not fall
nor that they won't be picked off by pea-shooters,
but that they won't fall apart from the will of God.

How often do we quote God's care for us
in the fact that he numbers every hair on our head . . .
But Jesus does not say that therefore we won't be among those
who, in the course of chemotherapy, will lose that hair:
only that God knows, and will never cease to care.

Shucks.

How often do we *not* quote the sword:
the fact that Jesus came *not* to bring unity at any price
but, on the contrary, division between truth and error,
good and evil and, should friends and brothers see it
from opposing sides, so be it.

How often do we *not* quote the daily need
gently but firmly to remove ourselves, again,
from the centre of our thinking and decision-making,
don our servant's apron and look to our Master
in unquestioning obedience . . .

Shucks.

To save my life
is to rate peace and quiet, and political correctness;
to judge the effect on my family and my pension plan,
to give in, rather than to give out;
to save my life
is to be sensible, and to play safe,
always to say 'Oh, I could never do that!' casting doubt
and therefore smothering the gift of God;
to save my life
is to keep my religion to myself
safe from accusations of intolerance, offending no one,
saving no one.
This is to save my life – and therefore to lose it.

To lose my life
is never, for the sake of peace or popularity
to deny the truth I've come to know; never to save my skin
with the silence which is compromise;
to lose my life
is never to look down at the path ahead and be deterred
by its demands: to look instead to the guide who promises
to see me through to the end;
to lose my life
is never to say no because the risk is too great,
because the risk of saying no, by decision or default

is always greater.
This is to lose my life – and therefore to save it.

Is there anywhere I would not go
is there anything I would not do
is there anyone I would not know
if he were to ask me?
Is there anywhere I would not live
is there anyone I would not leave
is there anything I would not give
if he were to ask me?

How do I know?
How do I know how fit I am to serve him?
I fear I have had too much comfort, too much distraction,
too little challenge;
I fear it has blurred my vision, sapped my strength,
scrambled my brain.

Jesus, help me to hear
not what I would like you to say
but what you *are* saying to me;
and make me fit,
fit enough, faithful enough, to follow
to follow hard
however hard.

Default Mode

Romans 6:12-13

You ask me, writer to the Romans, am I a slave to sin
or a slave to righteousness?

I only wish it were as easy as that;
I mean, I know which I would want to be
(*I'm a righteousness wannabe*, aren't we all? Well, perhaps not . . .)
But there's always this something in me
that wants to default back to some other mode
despite my best intentions.

Just like the computer.
I think I've got it all set up
with the right font and type size and margins
and then I turn it on one day and
surprise! It's reverted to comic sans; *come on,*
you know you always used to like me . . .

Or I decide to economise
and go for 10-point, and draft-print mode
(saves on cartridges);
but can I get it set as 'normal'?
Uh-uh. Every single time, I have to remember
to check it, reset it. Some slave.

Some slave. I have a horrible feeling
this is what God must be saying
about me. Quite good
at making all the right noises
but in practice, default
back to all the old ways.

Tell myself, be disciplined!
It won't hurt if you've had to miss lunch;
you don't need to eat that much . . .
But when I get back at ten to three
before I know it
I've made toast and tea.

Tell myself, stop opting out,
pretending you're in such a rush:
can't stop now, hope you're OK!
But before I've had time to give myself
a talking-to, I'm on my way, hurrying by
on the other side . . .

Tell myself, make time to pray
with your friends, when they call
for tea and sympathy; bring it to God!
But if I remember,
I tell myself they'll be embarrassed.
More often, I remember too late.

Whose slave, then?
Do my words, and my best intentions
carry the day?
Or do my actions, my stubborn
default mode, so often betray
my true allegiance?

And this is no academic,
philosophical quibble:
if the end of one
is eternal life and the end of the other,
death – that's a bit drastic.
I need to get this sorted.

I do not want to be
a false prophet, telling myself
'Peace! All is well!' when it isn't.

But neither do I want to be
berating myself for being simply
a work in progress.

Maybe it's the 'slave' mode
that's giving me trouble –
hardly politically correct;
'freedom of choice' is *de rigueur*
and mine's not giving in
without a considerable struggle

for there is a sense in which
I *do* need to choose each time
whose slave I wish to be;
that 'yes' of conversion, commitment,
does not mean that everything else
is a fait accompli.

And yet – there is a crucial difference.
As long as I am still
that *righteousness wannabe*
every later choice I make
is not about salvation – the *gift* of God,
counting me righteous – but holiness.

And as long as I have this debate
with myself, I keep good company:
Paul himself struggled
to do the good which he wanted,
resist the evil he hated,
deal with his 'body of death' default mode.

And take courage! I guess it's like
that annoying rule in Scrabble
when the value of the letters you're left with
is not only taken away from your score
but added to the score
of the one who finished first:

just so, every time I succeed
in making that righteous choice
it not only robs sin of a little more power
but adds that power to my faith
and I live in hope – no, in faith –
that one day the scales will tip

and righteousness become my default mode:
and that will be heaven.

Pulling Power

Romans 7:15-25a; Matthew 11:16-19, 25-30

Come to me,
all you who are weary and burdened,
and I will give you rest:
what a welcome invitation!
At the end of the road
a light in the window,
a hot bath, relaxation, the smell of bread,
time to off-load . . .

But what of the rest, after the rest?
We're so good at getting only half the story:
Take my yoke upon you,
and learn from me,
for my yoke is easy, and my burden light.
What a less welcome invitation is this?
To come, only in order to go?
To rest, only in order to go back to work?
Never, in this life,
to escape the obligation,
the yoke?

Not an everyday sight, nowadays,
unless you come from a third world country:
a pair of oxen, yoked together,
ploughing a furrow:

one ox can pull one ton,
but make the connection and two oxen,
it is said, can pull seven tons:
sounds like a good invention, the yoke

provided both want to go in the same direction:

but hardly a must-have accessory for us, nowadays.
Or is it?
Do we bow our necks to virtual yokes, which masquerade
in multiple disguises,
pulling us this way and that,
playing havoc with our better judgement?

All those things which seemed good to us,
which we embraced, eagerly
out of enthusiasm, or the need to belong,
or the need for a cause –
where are they pulling us?

In the trial of strength,
are they stronger, too strong,
a burden, a yoke, which we need to lay down?

Am I a fully paid-up, card-carrying
Tory, trade unionist, campaigner
for nuclear disarmament?
Freemason, football aficionado, friend of the earth?
When push comes to shove,
who has first call on my life?
Where am I bound?

I embraced my work,
grateful for income and skill;
but now my boss has my mobile number
the yoke has become a burden:
there's the rub.

I embraced my marriage,
grateful for friendship and love;
but now with children and ailing parents
the yoke has become a burden:
there's the rub.

I embraced my overdraft,
grateful for freedom to build and enjoy
but now with interest on store cards and loans
the yoke has become a burden:
there's the rub.

I am yoked to this philosophy
this therapy, this diet,
this debt; this initiative
this cause, this club, this code,
this guilt;
and they push me, and pull me
and I do not know what I want
and I do what I don't want to do
and what I want, I don't do;
so many call
and I am weary with it all,
weary and burdened
and my shoulders are sore,
rubbed raw.

But here is a tradesman who says
Come to me . . .
and he will ease these painful yokes from my shoulders
and pour on oil
and I can stretch my aching muscles, relax.
But though I lay down my yokes
casting my care upon him, for he cares for me,
this is only the first part of the story:
he won't let me lay down my responsibilities
for I would cease, then, to be a man.

No: as I watch, the carpenter
runs a practised hand and a skilled eye
over the discarded wood
and selects, and fashions a new, light, good yoke,
for him and me together
not overriding, for he is gentle and humble of heart;
never working against the grain

never pulling, but guiding,
him and me together;
rescuing all that is part of me,
responsibilities that remain mine,
commitments I'm called to keep
but each, now, in its proper place,
grafted into the carefully crafted wood that harnesses
him and me together.

But who is he,
this man who says
Come to me . . .
who promises me what only God can give,
who asks of me what a master would ask of his slave?
Do I trust him enough to take his yoke,
follow his lead, as we plough our furrow,
him and me together:
and find as we move earth
that we taste heaven?

Come to me . . .
Not for nothing did God,
knowing the need,
carve himself out a career as a carpenter:
bespoke furnishings –
yokes a speciality,
satisfaction guaranteed.

A Tale of Two Credit Cards

Romans 8:1-11

I am utterly non-plussed by debt.
It has always seemed to me that the world should-balance,
but somehow there seems to be too much on the debit side

and no-money seems to weigh heavier than money
dragging half the world into a well of misery
either through their own fault, or not;

for the rich nations borrow in order to lend
and are indebted for unnecessary consumables
and student education

while the poor nations borrow in order to live
and are indebted for their daily bread,
it seems, for ever:

so – please excuse my naivety –
since everyone appears to be in debt,
where does the money come from?

Is it constantly in circulation,
a convoluted economic double helix:
or does it lurk darkly at the bottom of an oil well?

How come, when my car refuses to run on empty
can the world continue to run, it seems,
on negative equity?

If all the debt in Britain were to be called in,
I understand, we'd be bankrupt in three weeks;
but we go on sawing away at the branch we're sitting on

and if all the debt in the world were to be called in,
what it would feel like then, as all the branches give way
and we all fall to the ground with a global crash?

Thank heaven there are glimmerings of hope
as some of the debts are cancelled, some of the world's poor
are allowed to tear up their IOUs;

just imagine – what unimaginable relief! – at last
to be able to teach, to heal, to do good; at last
to see the fruit of your labours, to build for the future!

But what of my debt? Buy now, pay later it said;
0 per cent finance; increase your overdraft,
go on, take out a loan – have it, you deserve it!

And I thought I had enough, was earning enough
to cover myself; after all, I worked hard and lived
in no more prodigal a fashion than the next

but now I find there is not enough, never enough
never ever enough in my account even to begin
to make an impression on that debt . . .

Aha! an advert offering to scoop up all my debts
and cover them with a single loan:
could this be my salvation?

Alas, I fear not: reading the small print,
paying off that loan may well be less complicated
but it's every bit as impossibly expensive;

if only – *if only* – it had been an advert offering
to scoop up all my debts and cover them,
cover them completely, write them off . . .

Dream on; this is the real world.
But it happened – it did, it happened! The offer
of a credit card *to cover all debt!*

Wait a minute – where's the catch? Let's read
the small print; bound to be a payback somewhere,
no such thing as a free lunch.

What does it say? 'There is now no burden of debt
for those who accept this Christ Jesus credit card;
the slate is wiped quite clean;

moreover, this card gives the holder free access
to all the wealth of heaven's store; please ask
the Holy Spirit for assistance.'

A store card! Is this, then, the catch?
With a Marks and Spencer card I can buy
only Marks and Spencer goods:

and with this card, I won't be able to buy
to feather my own nest, indulge my weaknesses
or get one up on my neighbour;

with this card, I can buy only what is in line
with the will of God, only the goods bought by his Son,
only the fruit of the Holy Spirit.

Did I say buy? No – he said it was free
and it has to be free: my account, my spiritual account
is empty, quite empty. I have earned – nothing.

Just imagine what unimaginable relief – at last
to be able to teach, to heal, to do good; at last
to enjoy the fruit of the Spirit, to build for the future!

Why, then, when I have signed up for such a golden card
do I often feel weighed down with obligation,
still burdened, confused, *condemned*?

A sign, I fear, that I find it hard to give up those other cards,
stop looking out for number one, resist temptation:
and so I go on running up debt after debt . . .

But as the Holy Spirit highlights each costly error,
this debt, too, I can submit, to be covered and written off:
this is *conviction*, repentance, receiving again a clean slate

unlike that vague *condemnation*, the voice that tells me
I am worthless: that is the work of the enemy
robbing, stealing, destroying both truth and joy.

If I am to walk the way of the Spirit, then let me submit
to that plastic surgery – cut up those other cards
and learn to depend on Jesus alone;

but know that while I wait for the Spirit
to finish his work in me, I am hidden in Christ: it is he
who has set me free and I *will* believe his word

he who took the spiritual debt of the world
and crossed it out, once and for all:
for all, including me.

The Organic Gardener

Romans 8:12-25; Matthew 13:24-30, 36-43

Last year they decommissioned a block of flats in the next street.
It used to be elderly only; now, it's first come, first served.
And they were not happy! No, not at all.
I mean, don't know who you might get!
Single mums with squalling children. Loud music.
Unemployed thugs with tattoos. Drugs.

And they were quite right. They did. Get them all.

I took Dot for coffee. 'Nice to get out, dear!
Used to be such a nice, quiet, decent-living place; now,
never a moment's peace. Don't go out on my own any more;
one of those men might be hanging round the stairs,
and they give me the creeps, they do: them and their tattoos.
No, I just keep my door shut and mind my own business.'

She takes cake, but does not meet my eye.

'Why did they have to do it, anyway?
Why not give them their own flats, and let us have ours?
I don't say it's always their own fault, mind –
probably come from broken homes,
parents that don't know any better –
but why mix them in with the likes of us?'

I feel sad for Dot.

Most of us sometimes wish we could craft
a cosy corner, away from the cold winds,
the mud and blood; where the music would be
gentle, the children dutiful and bright;

we would hear only good news
and everything in the garden would be lovely.

But I also feel sad about Dot.

She used to be such a lovely Christian lady;
taught the Sunday School for years,
helped with the luncheon club and the church fête;
but now, somehow, her faith has shrivelled
like a fragile flower in a late frost
into something small, and brown and moribund:

she seems to have shrunk.

Then there was Charlie. We met in the park.
He'd signed the petition, too;
nicely worded, nothing personal, but quite firm:
not in my back yard (or block of flats).
We fought in the war: for goodness' sake,
don't we deserve a bit of peace now?

I feel sad for Charlie.

Kept himself to himself, for the most part.
Occasionally came to church: not sure
whether he actually believed it all or not.
But I tell you what surprised me: when I saw him,
that day in the park, he was sitting on a bench
next to a kid with tattoos. Chatting.

This is interesting.

'Hallo, Charlie.' I sit down. 'How're you doing?'
'Oh, not so bad. You met Andy here?'
'Hi. You from the flats?' He nods.
'Next door,' says Charlie. 'He's doing it up.
One of these days, I'll get my stepladder back!'
'End of the month,' says Andy; 'promise, mate!'

'He's not a bad lad,' Charlie tells me later.
'Starting work next month, down the nurseries;
mum gets new boyfriend, he gets chucked out of home;
can't get a job till he gets an address,
you know how it goes. Not easy for some kids.'
'Good thing he's got a good neighbour now,' I say.

'Only doing the Christian thing,' he mutters.

I look at him again, in his anonymous
elderly widower's wear, correct but drab, worn;
how fearfully easy it is to assume
he is winding down now, the good times
behind him; but something is going on,
inside something new is springing to life . . .

I do not feel sad about Charlie.

He seems to have grown.

'Would you sign that petition again?'
I ask him one day. 'I don't know,' he says.
I can hear the music from next door,
had to squeeze past the pram in the hallway.
But the two-year-old calls him grandad
and Andy has planted his window boxes

and Charlie shakes his head. 'I don't know.
Cosy is fine if all we want is to die in peace,
but maybe there's more to it than that.
Who's to say what good may come? Weeds
may turn out to be flowers, and flowers, weeds.
Maybe we should just trust the Almighty more.'

Maybe we should.

Trust the organic gardener.

Verdict

Romans 8:26-39

CP – Counsel for the Prosecution; CD – Counsel for the Defence.

CP Would you like to give the court your name?

Defendant Everyman

CP You are charged with crimes against king and country; how do you plead?

Everyman Not guilty

CP Not guilty! An extraordinary plea, if I may say so, in the light of such overwhelming evidence.

Judge You may not say so; that is up to you to demonstrate, and the court to decide.

CP Your Honour. I will base my case on the simple fact that a subject of the king should obey the laws of that kingdom; no one, I think, could argue with that.

Judge Proceed.

CP May I remind you of the first law, the foundation on which everything else rests: you shall love the Lord your God with all your heart, soul, mind and strength. I submit, Everyman, that you have broken this law every day of your life: that you don't even know what it means, to give yourself so completely to anyone or anything, let alone someone you know so sketchily, so distantly. And to make him Lord – the one with whom you have merely a nodding acquaintance on a Sunday? This is no more than lip service.

Judge Can you give specific examples?

CP Hundreds, Your Honour. If he is ill, does he pray? No, he first rushes to the medicine cupboard, the books of alternative therapies, the surgery; does he make time in his day to spend with the one he says he loves the most? No, he busies himself from morning to night, with only a quick glance or a desperate prayer to his 'Lord'. Does he care enough for the honour of God to speak out against all that dishonours him, or to tell his neighbour the good news? No, tolerance and tact are his excuses, and he speaks of good fortune rather than the goodness of God. When things go wrong, is he at peace, trusting God implicitly? No, he is dejected and questions whether God still cares.

Judge   Is this true?

Everyman   Yes, Your Honour.

CP   *(Surprised)* He cannot deny it! I can only imagine, then, that it is the second law of the kingdom with which he hopes to redeem himself: you shall love your neighbour as yourself. But I would submit, Your Honour, that here too he is guilty: albeit more in the omission than in the observance.

Judge   For example?

CP   He does not even know who lives in his street: yes, he will respond to a request, gladly: lend a spanner, feed the cat; but he has not knocked, chatted, invited, offered, cared. He has not tried to seek out the lonely, the poor, the need. When he shops: yes, he will make a gesture, buy as ethically as possible; but he has not seriously thought about carbon footprints or radical, simple living that puts the world's poor and one's own grandchildren first. He is nice enough, and always ready to help (though he's glad people can't see what he is thinking about them): but at the end of the day, number one comes first, doesn't it?

Judge   Does it?

Everyman   Yes, Your Honour.

CP   Your Honour, on his own admission the defendant has broken the two cardinal laws of the kingdom. No matter, then, that he hasn't committed murder or, to my knowledge adultery or serious fraud. He is therefore guilty, and deserves his sentence: that he must live only until he dies, and that death will put an end to his chances of life with God, for which he was created but for which he is utterly unworthy.

Judge   If you admit, Everyman, that you have broken the laws of the kingdom, why then do you plead 'Not guilty'?

CD   On my advice, Your Honour.

Judge   Proceed.

CD   That dishonourable gentleman, the Counsel for the Prosecution, knows full well of his own guilt in handing my client this rope to hang himself.

Judge   Your plea is then diminished responsibility?

CD   By no means. Everyman is responsible for his own actions and must take the consequences.

Judge   What, then?

CD   The laws of which my adversary speaks are essential, but impossible; not only my client, but the whole human race must stand convicted.

CP   Yes, yesss!!

CD   Convicted first and foremost of crimes towards the one who created them for so much more, the one whom they have betrayed, whose power they sought to usurp, whose image they have desecrated, whose love they have doubted and denied. Crimes against God himself.

CP   Arguably the most serious charge of all!

CD   Indeed. And no question but that the verdict would be 'guilty' and the sentence, that death of which you spoke.

CP   Would be?

CD   The charge has been made, the verdict passed, the death died.

CP   What? When? Who?

CD   Before the foundation of the world, God charged himself with finding a way to reconcile justice and mercy. He stood in that dock. He received the sentence. He fed death a richer feast than death could ever have hoped for: and it proved more than death could stomach. Death need no longer be

	the end! I have the scars to prove it. Everyman is free to live!
Judge	Are you telling me there's no case to be answered?
CD	That's right. It's past history.
Judge	And what do you say, you who bring these accusations?
CD	*(Looks round)* He seems to have left the court. Come, Everyman.

To the Manna Born

Isaiah 55:1-5; Matthew 14:13-21

I guess you could have made men
who were never hungry
or were happy to live on pills;
but how unsatisfying
never to smell bread baking,
never to use our skills
to hunt, or fish, or grow food:
never to taste and see that God is good.

I guess you could have made men
who were never hungry
for you, lacking all spirit;
but how unsatisfying
for us, never to grow through wonder,
or worship; and what merit
for you, to have one more brute beast
instead of sons and daughters to share your feast?

Yes, you could have made men
such as these; but in your wisdom
you chose otherwise,
blessed us with incompleteness,
healthy appetite
and a spirit which cries
for bread, and breadth and depth of purpose:
that you would earth, and then unearth us.

And so that we should not forget
that we who are little lower than the angels
are also dust
and we who eat and sleep and breed and die

also see visions
our twin hungers must,
like our twin natures, interweave:
if we would eat, we should also believe . . .

In the beginning, when Adam and Eve
were hungry, you gave them
a garden: Eden,
with fruit of every colour,
taste, nutritional value, texture
they could feed on;
but also, your divine providence
offered them their soul's food: obedience.

Feed flesh and spirit,
bite the firm flesh of fig or grape,
feast on their juice
but also take into themselves your words,
willingly, submissively
or else they cut loose
from all that makes them fully human; why
eat, only to survive – and die?

In the wilderness, when the Israelites
were hungry, you gave them
bread from heaven,
manna, there, right on the doorstep,
with double rations on day six
and so, rest on day seven;
but you also asked that no one collect more
than a day's ration, or try to make a store:

sufficient unto the day is the manna thereof.
Eat, drink and enjoy;
but trust your word
that you will provide for tomorrow,
trust you, for you planted the whole earth;
see how absurd
it would be for you simply to feed
their bodies, and neglect their soul's need . . .

And in that other desert, when five thousand men
were hungry, having brought
their sick and dying
to seek healing, Jesus gave them
not only food for the body,
multiplying
their scant resources, but the unforgettable
experience of miracle,

telling us, in so many words,
not to look at our own poverty
but at his riches;
blessed are those who hunger
and thirst not just for food
and drink, which is
quite understandable,
but also for right living, which is more laudable.

Still to come, the upper room, where they met
to eat the Passover meal
and Jesus took bread
feeling his own body breaking,
his own blood spilling,
thinking ahead
to the terrible prising apart of body and soul:
to the rising from death to make us whole,

saying, in so many words,
'You look for the return of manna as a sign
of your Messiah:
but this is no one-off manna miracle:
I am the living bread come down
from heaven: all I require
is that you remember – do not live by earthly food
alone, but by every word, or Word of God.'

There is so much hunger in the world,
so much appetite
unsatisfied

for bread, and circuses
for full bellies, for minds at rest,
for tears dried
and the aid agencies do their best
and sometimes bread and wine is blessed

and in the gift we glimpse the giver,
manna born in Bethlehem,
house of bread.
What is it? Who is it? Christ, who provides
himself enough to whet our appetite
for the banquet spread
in heaven, for his heavenly bride:
in heaven where body and soul, at one, are satisfied.

After Everest

1 Kings 19:9-18; Matthew 14:22-33

I guess you have to feel for Elijah.
I mean, what do you *do*
once you've managed Chelsea
scaled Everest
sailed the Atlantic single-handed
trounced 400 prophets of Baal?

Yes, you have to feel sorry
for those who have made it
to the top: for whom the only way is
down.
How can the rest of life
fail to be anticlimax?

It's hard to get away from the idea
that life should *progress,*
however much the evidence
proves it is a series
of highs and lows,
ups and downs

and the only thing that *may* progress
is character.

The Bible – along with every other book,
newspaper or TV show –
majors, of course
on the exceptional.
'Dog not lost'
is hardly news.

And Elijah seems to hurtle
from one drama to the next,
adrenalin junkie:
coming down to earth now
with a bump
and severe withdrawal symptoms;

alongside Moses,
greatest of the prophets:
running away! Throwing
what sounds suspiciously like a tantrum
because it's all gone
pear-shaped.

So many miracles he'd seen!
Miracles of food, of healing;
miracles of fire, of supernatural strength –
and for what?
A prophet without honour;
a nation without repentance.

I don't know which is worse:
to believe in miracles
but never to have seen one
and become resigned
to living, it would seem,
in an unbelieving Nazareth

or to have commanded rain
and seen the fire fall,
the dead raised:
and realise
that miracles – surely God's trump card? –
do not win the game.

I mean, *why* the wind,
the earthquake and the fire?
Simply to prove
that God was *not* in them?

That sometimes less is more?
Perhaps so.

Elijah flees to the rock
where God met Moses;
surely here, if anywhere
(at the Bible week, the retreat centre)
he will recover his anointing?
Perhaps not.

'What are you doing *here*, Elijah?
Waiting for another miracle?
Why?
To prove that I am a God of miracles?
But you already know that,
you, of all people.

'Why?
Miraculously to convict the Israelites?
But you already know
that doesn't work.
They have such short memories
and I look for settled faith.

'Why?
To vindicate your own career?
But you already know
that prophets are unpopular:
comes with the territory.
Sorry.

'So what are you doing *here*, Elijah?
My word is always near
to all who fear me
though sometimes it may sound
like gentle silence . . .
Go back the way you came, find me again

in an ordinary obedience,
a daily working out of holiness
not on the mountain tops
but in the plains
where most of my non-mountaineers
work out their little lives . . . '

It makes sense: that ordinarily
God is in the ordinary.

I could wish for another storm on the lake,
where the waves are not stilled
and no one comes walking on water;
but they recognise God
in the build of the boat
and the strength and the skill of the boatmen.

But perhaps I'm just jealous
because my prayers for miracles sink without trace

and, like Elijah, I feel I've hit burn-out;
all that I've strived for eludes my grasp
and there's no more strength,
and the pity is all for myself.
But then comes the whisper,
'Go back the way you came,

'go back to the ground of your faith, Elijah:
Yahweh is God!
If I call you to walk on water,
come!
If not, stay in the boat
and I will help you catch fish, and men;
I will help you mend nets, and quarrels;
I will help you to weather storms
and pour oil on troubled waters;
I will smile at you from the eyes of children,
reprove you in the words of the wise;
I will teach you to love the unlovely

and swim against the tide of indifference;
I will have no need of miracles
to keep you busy,
or amaze you,
or to achieve all that needs to be done.'

After Everest,
the heights of godliness,

where to go down
can be to progress

and life is hardly an anticlimax
but a miracle in itself.

Overruled

Matthew 15:10-28

I think that's what got to me in the end
that we were so busy monitoring our customer service
that we never noticed
when our customer, worn down with frustration,
decided to end it all:
relationship ruled out.

Tick the box, time the call,
trail the audit;
fill the forms, spin the stats,
top the targets

and never mind the empty hall,
the writing on the wall.

Today's Pharisees, downloading yesterday's
who were so busy safeguarding God's service
that they never noticed
when the people, worn down with frustration,
decided to end it all;
death by overkill.

Tithe the cumin, double the fast,
treble the prayer;
keep it kosher, ask permission to breathe
on the Lord's day

and never mind that God will chart
not our appearance, but our heart.

Why? Why, why, why am I doing all this religious *stuff*?

Because it is easier to draw up a rule, throw up a wall
and know, but prefer to ignore, that what keeps me safe inside
will keep others out?

Because it is easier to mark a list, to check what I must do,
and know, but choose not to see, that my doing hides
my lack of being?

Because it is easier to sign up, and go through the motions
and know, but refuse to admit, it is duty not heart: split
personality?

If this is true, one day
either I will crack, or heart will win, and I will drift away.

When I set out on my long-distance life's walk
of course I take the guide book,
having glanced through it first: I'm not one to leave things to chance.

There are basic rules – please shut the gate,
where there is livestock, keep your dog on a lead;
clear up after aforementioned creature; don't leave litter
and follow the waymarked paths. So far, so good.
But there are times when the paths and the signs disappear
and the book is frustratingly silent . . .

I think now that is how it is meant to be.
If it was overruled, if the book had every detail –
'Climb the stile and walk two hundred metres along the left-hand hedge;
follow the gravel path past the cowshed, turn right by the sycamore
    tree' –
I'd spend the entire walk with my nose in the book,
    never see the view, and feel my heart moved
    never scan the horizon, or know my spirit soar
    never realise the one I meet is lost and cold
    never make a decision, and therefore grow
    never trust the one whose hand I hold
        who wrote the book.

And that is the point of my long-distance walk:
not just that I should make it to the end, having dutifully closed the gates
but that I have been broken and blessed
by all the bleakness and beauty that it offers, and more –
that I shall have fallen in love with the one whose hand I hold,
who admits the walk was just an excuse to spend time with me,
to awaken my love, to propose
that we should be together, enjoy one another, for ever
   the one who wrote the book,
   the guidebook, the rules
simply to keep me in earshot of him, my lover.

The Pharisees kept the rules
and were ruled by the rules:
people of the book.
Jesus kept the rules
but was ruled by the Spirit
of God's grace.
The Gentile woman knew no rules
but sensed the Spirit:
test case . . .

Rules – or relationship?
Relationship without rules,
spoken or unspoken, will
die;
but even more surely,
rules without relationship
kill.

Jesus knew
there are rules, and there are rules:
rules rooted in the very nature of God
woven into the very fabric of creation
which must stand
if the world is not to become unravelled;
and rules which relate to a time,
and a realm, and a land

which may – which must – be overruled
if the world is not to become untravelled.

Where letter and spirit conflict,
let the Spirit prevail
and rewrite the script.

Knowing Me, Knowing You

Romans 12:1-8; Matthew 16:13-20

Remember the TV series? Brilliant title.
Like Alice in Wonderland: 'You?' said the caterpillar; 'Who are *you*?'

Who am I?

In some ways, you have all too much information about me,
can identify me in so many ways, card or no card:
I have a National Insurance number, an employee number, a credit/debit
   and a few store card numbers, a film society and a leisure centre
   membership number, (oh, and a few raffle ticket numbers);
I am known by my fingerprint, the iris of my eye and my blood group;
you can find my number in the phone book and my email address at
   hotmail;
you can even see my photo on my passport and my driving licence

but what does all this add up to? You can identify me, I fear all too easily;
but do you *know* me? Do *I* know me?

Who am I?
You must tell me, because *I am* only in relation to you.
(Only God is simply, uniquely, *I am*.)

I am – a son
because I recognise that you are my mother, my father;
but how am I *son*?
Is it significant? How does it shape my life, how does it grow me?

I am – a brother
because I recognise that you are my brother, sister;
but how am I *brother*?
How do I support, encourage, agree and differ? Am I your keeper?

I am – a husband
because I recognise that you are my wife;
but how am I *husband*?
How do I love, 24/7? Is this my raison d'etre?

I am – a teacher
because I recognise that you are my pupil;
but how am I *teacher*?
How does it inspire me, to inspire another? Is this my forte?

I am – a convict
because I recognise that you have judged me guilty of crime;
but how am I *convict*?
How do my guilt and imprisonment challenge me? Make or unmake me?

I am – a sportsman
because I recognise that you are my team;
but how am I *sportsman*?
How does the skill, the thrill, the togetherness satisfy me?

I am all of these, and more; I am legion. Every new relationship
shows me, or develops in me
a new facet, and I discover that I am,
also, *this*.

What, then, defines me? *Who am I?*

'Who do you say that I am?' asked Jesus
and Peter told him.
'Son of Man': could mean everything or nothing – you decide;
it is always up to you to decide.
'Christ' – anointed, prophet, priest and king; that was a first for Jesus:
you're the one we've all been waiting for.
'Son of the living God': wow, pretty dramatic, that:
begotten, not made.

But what's this? As Peter understands now
who Jesus is, so he discovers too, for the first time,
who Peter is: glimpses how
this new relationship will be the making of him, mould the clay

of stormy fisherman and fire him to solid rock;
this is who he is:
firm foundation, founding father of the Church
which will remain, against all odds, embodying
the spirit of that same Jesus
until he comes again.

And who am I?

Perhaps it's only Jesus who can tell me,
who can access all the detail held on that divine database
(not numbers; no, I think not: *essentials*.)
And perhaps it is only as I know him
that I also know myself . . .

I am – a sinner
because I recognise that Jesus calls himself my saviour
and I am learning to see that I am not holy, learning to be forgiven:
and I am – humbled.

I am – a friend of God
because I recognise that Jesus now calls me his friend
and I am learning to dare to draw near to God:
and I am – comforted.

I am – a lamb
because I recognise that Jesus calls himself my shepherd
and I am learning what it means to be nurtured and secure:
and I am – released.

I am – a branch
because I recognise that Jesus calls himself the vine
and I am learning, slowly, to allow his spirit to grow fruit in me:
and I am – quieted.

I am – a disciple
because I recognise that Jesus is my Lord and Master
and I am learning how much I have to learn, and to put faith into action:
and I am – challenged.

I am – is this, in the end, who I am? – a child of God
because I recognise that Jesus gives power to all who believe to become
   children of God
and, believing, I am – reborn
and I am learning, oh, so slowly it seems!
to be a child,
growing;
knowing you, God my father;
knowing me, God, your child
growing more like you
knowing more what it means to be me

and it will be heaven
to know you fully
and in that clear recognition, for the first time
to see my clear reflection
and know fully, as I am fully known: finally
to know who I am.

Idol Speculation

Romans 12:9-21; Matthew 16:21-28

My god is dead.

How about yours?
I think he must be dead too.
And good riddance, I say!

Caesarea Philippi was full of them,
dead gods; idols, shrines –
oh, and Herod's great temple to Caesar.
He wasn't dead, of course;
but god? Heaven help us.
Gods from wood, precious metal, stone,
richly gilded, beautifully made, persuasively marketed
but dead. All dead.
Lying idols
lying idle. All dead.

Except for one, the one
who chose Caesarea, of all places,
to ask his disciples,
'Who do you say I am?' and to hear Peter's exclamation:
'You are the Messiah,
the Son of the living God!'

And Jesus applauded, owned
that moment of revelation;
nevertheless, forbade
their too-ready tongues, knowing
they were not, in fact, ready to understand
what they'd seen, would misunderstand
the living God

iconoclast
who confounds expectation,
defies speculation.

And sure enough, Peter,
paving the way for the rest of us,
takes it upon himself to tell God
what he should and should not do
if he is to live up to our expectations,
to our image of him.

How blessed he was indeed to be called Satan!
To be stopped in his tracks before his idle words created an idol.

For we all fall for idols,
even we who say we believe in God,
for it is 'my god' I believe in.
My god, who would tolerate everything
except hell; who would excuse everyone
except the religious right
(whom he would doubtless consign to hell, if it existed).
My god, whom I think I glimpse
in a September sunset,
sense in the spine-tingling symphony
which swoops and soars amid the fan-vaulting
of the great cathedral; my god who,
however, does not have much to say
about moral imperatives
or – heaven forbid! – sin.

And your god? You tell me
god is inside you, that life force
you share with the whole of creation,
which pulses through every living thing
and sleeps in the very stones.
You are a spiritual man, yes:
but you speak of energy, harmony, balance
and being at one with the world. Your god
is not personal, does not speak, nor hear,

nor forgive;
nor is there anything to forgive
except ignorance, and clumsiness
and noise.

But I fear
that my god does not exist
any more than yours
except as a comforting illusion,
an illusion of comfort
born of a need for comfort,
a need for illusion.
I fear
that when I have the presumption
to ask that idle question;
'What do I make of God?'
I have in mind not the things of God
but the things – the needs, the prejudice –
of men.

I fear
I should ask, rather,
'What does God – the God who IS,
if indeed he is –
make of me?'

For God
is not the teacher who gives us a blank sheet of paper
and asks us to draw our idea of god;
nor the one who points up and out to nature
and asks us to wonder at it, to become one with it;
nor the one who points inward
and asks us to find divinity in the depth of our being.
No.
God is the one who intrudes into the world
this Jesus;
demanding 'Who do you say I am?'
demanding an answer

and, like everyone else
(not least my husband, my boss, my son)
he is who he is,
not who I'd like him to be.

I fear
I must take up my cross and deny myself
the right to create them in my own image
and then, like Peter, remonstrate
when they fail to live up to it.
No: each one, even God
supremely God
has the right to say
I AM WHO I AM
and what are the rest of you going to do about it?

My god is dead
and yours is too;
all our selective, customised, idolised gods
are dead:

but God is not dead.

He is unexpected
controversial
extreme
painful, joyful
uncomfortable strong comfort
more like Jesus than we dare dream
and true

and, unlike Nietzsche,
alive and well.

OK Corral

Romans 13:8-14

OK, we all agree it's cool,
  'Love your neighbour as yourself':
the golden rule.
And most of us are quick to claim
we do our best to stick to what it says –
but do we? Or do we fool ourselves,
really?

If the truth were only known,
I do not *really* love myself, let alone
my neighbour: and that is largely why I do not
really
love my neighbour.

Don't I love myself?
Indulge myself, yes –
put my own pleasure, profit, reputation first;
assume, somehow, I am my greatest treasure: I'm OK, Jack!
But is this love?
Love seeks always the highest good: is this really it?
Surely I *lack* love
when I always give myself the benefit of any doubt,
ruling out honesty;
always make excuses for my faults,
ruling out growth;
always take centre stage, sideline
my neighbour who waits in the wings
assume, somehow, he is not fine, not OK?

Sometimes, though, it's the other way round;
for whatever reason, nature or nurture,

I am so hard on myself: I'm not OK!
Extravagant, greedy, idle, dumb –
I judge myself, and am found wanting.
Is this love?
Is it good to call myself a worm,
I who am made in the image of God?
Is it good to see myself as useless scum, when Christ says
'Come! Through me, you can do all things'?
Nor is it love always to see my neighbour through rose-tinted glasses,
always to excuse her faults,
assume, somehow, she is always OK
and I must defer,
in some obscure kind of penance.

And then there's the worst of all possible worlds
when nothing and no one is ever OK,
when I am a worm and my neighbour's a louse,
when judgement obliterates love
   and gloom descends on the house;
when I deny the prevailing goodness of God
and credit the devil
with victories he does not deserve.
Is this love?
Even-handed, I grant you,
but scorpions for fish
and stones for bread.

How, then, can it ever be OK
to see myself as OK
when I know too much,
when I know what I do that nobody sees,
when I know what I say that nobody hears,
when I know what I think that nobody even suspects?
How, then, can I ever love myself in a way
that would model a love for my neighbour
(the one I rush to meet,
and the one I cross the street to avoid):
a love that makes the golden rule

really
work
OK?

I am OK
because I sprang from the thought, and the heart
and the plan of God
and I am not his first mistake.
I am not OK, though,
because in a thousand ways I distort
his image in me.
I am OK, though,
because you are at work in me, Jesus,
to forgive, and heal, and make new
and you will not give up on me
until I am
really
OK

and you, my neighbour – you are OK
because you, too, sprang from the thought, and the heart
and the plan of God
and neither are you his first mistake.
You are not OK, though,
because in a thousand ways you distort
his image in you.
You *can* be OK, though,
if only you will let Jesus work in you,
to forgive, and heal, and make new;
for he will not give up on you
until you are
really
OK

and this will be my love for myself,
always to let Jesus have his way in me,
seeking my highest good

and this will be my love for you, my neighbour,
always to pray, and so to be and do, that Jesus will have his way in you,
for this is to seek *your* highest good

we are the same, you and I:
utterly inspired, utterly hopeless –
and utterly redeemable!
OK?
I'll say.

Heart Trouble

Matthew 18:21-35

My aunt
cheated me out of my inheritance, you know;
Queen Anne silver, no less.
To say that I've not spoken to her since would be misleading
as I never spoke to her much before,
having been warned off by another relative, who said
she'd seen better forms of life under stones.

My aunt, though,
she *was* family, and we all know we don't choose our family:
they're a 'given',
not just for my benefit, but for theirs: not just to provide
food, a bed, a shoulder to cry on but a small world in which to grow
compassion, understanding, forgiveness:
all that would make me fully human . . .

She cheated me.
Oh how quick I am to jump to defend my rights,
to pick up arms;
I am so much less likely to stop and think 'Why?
What need was there in her, for kudos, acceptance – hardly for money –
that made *things* more important than people? Surely I should feel
not anger, but the sadness for her that leads to forgiveness?

Queen Anne silver.
Come on now, girl: what would you have done with silver?
Moaned about the insurance.
Of course, it wasn't the silver but the *principle* of the thing . . .
Oh how easy it is to fall into exactly the same trap:
principles before people, get on my high horse;
as if my own behaviour were beyond reproach!

So we're not speaking.
Sounds like a couple of kids in the playground: usually, though
they manage to sort it out.
Of course I'll always be closer to some of the family than others
but to close a door – to cut off communication,
to cut off circulation, is a kind of sclerosis: hardening
of spiritual arteries, symptom of heart disease.

And listening to gossip.
If gossip be the food of prejudice, how vital – and how hard –
to close our ears.
I should not judge at all: least of all, pre-judge.
Rumour, misunderstanding, half-truth: the temptation to agree,
acquire an ally, is sweet – but sickly sweet;
blood poisoning.

And what is writ small
in the workings or non-workings of my family
is also writ large
in the divisions of community into old-timer and immigrant,
each with its social calendar and pub;
in the splitting of a land by race, ethnicity, past history –
and, of course, in the church

which at best
is a more or less dysfunctional family – family, nonetheless –
and at worst
a battleground littered with debris from the cold war.
How often would our Lord, our great physician diagnose
heart trouble? That we have not loved enough, or cared enough
to heed the warning signs.

He comes asking
not just that you and I should seek to honour him
but for a *community*
which dares to own the hurt given and received;
which dares confront wrongs said and thought and done
which is learning to be open, and to forgive;
whose love for one another dazzles the world.

And what does he find,
the great physician, when he examines us?
Classic symptoms.
High blood pressure. Issues unresolved, hyper-tension, anger.
Breathlessness. A long time since windows were open to the wind of the
    Spirit.
Pain, and avoidance of pain, by whatever means.
And a slow, creeping paralysis.

There is the risk
as arteries, and attitudes harden, that not enough oxygen
circulates
to get rid of the waste, the debris of bad feeling,
and blood clots and limits the body's effectiveness
or, worse, blocks the messages from the brain which say 'Forgive!'
and kills, then, at a stroke.

So, Aunt,
I would like to say 'I forgive you for taking my silver; if it means so
    much to you,
you're welcome to it.
And forgive me my resentment, and my cold shoulder.'
And to you, sister, who poisoned my mind against her,
I would like to say 'I forgive you too. And forgive me for not urging you
to find a better way . . . '

I would like to.
But I have left it too late.
Heart disease kills.

Fair Enough

Jonah 3:10–4:11; Matthew 20:1-16

It's one of the first things most of us remember being told:
'You'll just have to get used to the fact
that life's not fair!
That you always have hand-me-down trainers
that the pantomime got cancelled
the tooth fairy had a night off
chocolate makes your hair fall out
and I know you wanted the red one, but Jason's mum can't cope
    when he throws a tantrum . . .'

OK, so life's not fair;
but why can't it be equally unfair to everyone?

We can be such a strange, perverse people:
I'm sad when you are low and then life seems to kick you when you're
    down;
I'm downright aggrieved when the same thing happens to me.
But there's a nasty, sneaky bit of me
(which I'd rather not admit to)
which is also a little aggrieved when life seems to shower you
    with undeserved blessings,
silver spoons in the mouth,
bread with butter *and* jam, and cake;
and I discover that it's not that easy
truly to rejoice with those that rejoice.
Why you? Why not me?

And when the undeserved blessings are mine?
The danger is that I come to see them as deserved
because others have had them too (being no more deserving)

so it's only fair that I have my share;
or because I have suffered my fair share of unfairness,
so I deserve some kind of compensation, after all.

The more I think about 'fair'
the more I begin to see that it is not quite the noble concept I thought.
A fair deal, justice for all – what could be wrong about that?
And yet I sense, there *is* something about it
that is grudging and penny-pinching, poor
and flat, and cold, and hard
that cramps the spirit
and clamps the heart:
just so much – and no more.

Fair
is also far too complex and controversial;
is it fair that you should earn more than I
because you are a top advertising executive and I am a second chef?

Yes, you have a better brain, letters after your name;
but I have more common sense, and more skills;
you have the higher rent, and the daily commute
but I have the antisocial hours, and the kitchen's heat;
you have the satisfaction of soaring sales
but whilst they don't have to buy gizmos, people must eat.

And you were born with your brain, and I was born with mine
(what there is of it)
and you were born on the right side of the river
and I was born quick but dyslexic

and you have two incomes and no kids
and I have four boys and an overdraft:
is that fair?

but that's our choice,
isn't it?
Is it?

And if earthly rewards are a vexed question,
how about heaven?
Will St Peter also find himself perplexed?
Will it be fair that your credentials persuade,
that heaven's door opens for you
but not for me
or indeed, controversially, for me and not for you?
Your dad's a vicar, and you go to church
(from habit or conviction?)
You have a sponsor child in Tanzania
(easier than the chaos of your own? – whatever)
Your life is free from scandal
(did you have the chance?)
Your case will be as good as most they hear:
a fair chance, I'd say.

But me – I'm not a bit religious
(too many dry words and collection plates)
can barely clothe and feed my own kids
(though they're happy enough, and close);
looking back, I ain't been no saint
(I'd be the first to admit).
So if he turns me away, I guess I'd have to say
fair enough.

But no – that wouldn't be fair,
either way;
God isn't planning to spend eternity
sorting out shades of grey.
Being God,
he's come up with a new take on 'fair':
kicks all the confusion clean into touch . . .

A whole denarius for a day's work,
that was super-generous,
over and above what any of them deserved.
How much more, heaven:
over and above what any of us could ever deserve
so forget it!

Forget the early nights and the gift aid,
low energy lights and prayers prayed;
forget the long hours, the sacrifice made;
forget the special powers, the accolades:
I'm afraid
no qualification qualifies;
no justification justifies.
At the gates of heaven
the wind whips all words and works away
and all stand equally empty-handed,
having earned nothing,
learned nothing,
stranded
on the mercy of God

which is utterly fair,
asking of all alike
only the willingness to be
on the receiving end
of grace:
free
for all.

No, life's not fair: but God
is equally,
gloriously unfair
to everyone.

Not a Leg to Stand On

Philippians 2:1-13

It's one of those verses that stops you in your tracks;
in a medieval manuscript, it would have been illuminated
(or in today's version, the word document,
would have that annoying paper clip dancing up and down at you)
such is its stupendous claim:
  at the name of Jesus, every knee will bow
  and every tongue confess him Lord.

Lord, does that mean the gang at school who locked the 'Holy Joes' in
  the loo?

And my friend's dad who wouldn't let him go to church because he said
  it was brainwashing, and he should have outgrown Father Christmas?

And the medical researchers who take it upon themselves to customise
  our ethics?

And the philosophers and scientists who long ago 'proved' you were no
  more than a tale told by so many idiots?

And what about Hitler and Stalin and all the world's dictators who
  usurp your role but create hell on earth?

Will they be kneeling there? All of them?
In penitence? In worship?
Or felled to their knees by your irresistible glory, but grudging,
impenitent?

And Lord, does that mean all those who know your name only as a
  swear word?

And those who talk of you with sweet reasonableness, granting your
    gifted teaching but denying your deity?

And what about those journalists who can't bear to miss any opportunity
    to snipe at religion and are highly selective in their reporting?

And what of those of us who muddy the waters for others because our
    lives belie our words and so we, too, take your name in vain?

Will our tongues confess your name together? All of us?
In revelation? In praise?
Or faced, and forced, by unpalatable truth
which we cannot deny?

These verses – arresting, yes;
but they disturb me, slamming my emotions
now into fast forward,
now into neutral,
now into reverse.

Now into fast forward:
jubilant, expectant , I can't wait to see what it will be like,
Jesus in all his glory, King of kings, Lord of lords
and everything sorting itself out, settling,
finally finding its true place and purpose,
creation itself redeemed,
its groaning turned into a great shout of welcome
as its creator, the Word of God, comes into his own,
his own inheritance
and all the unanswered questions are seen to be
irrelevant
as, for the first time, we really *see*.

Now into neutral:
pulling me back to the present,
checking the state of my own heart,
that it won't be smug,
'I told you so!'
'See, I was right after all!'
or covering a secret self-righteousness

with a cloak of seeming pure delight;
reminding me of the sheer grace of God, which alone
enables me to look forward to such a day
with awe, not terror: which alone
pulls the carpet of pride
from under my own feet . . .

Now into reverse:
an even greater sobering,
realising these verses do not speak of a whole world saved
and they all lived happily ever after
but of responsibility: mine.
My responsibility, to love, and so to live and speak
to the hurting and the hurtful,
to the atheist, the agnostic and the apathetic,
to the self-sufficient and the suicidal,
to all the children of this world, if they would also be
children of the next:
before it is too late.

At the name of Jesus, every knee shall bow –
in heaven
could we want more proof, that Jesus is also God?
for surely, in heaven, God alone is worshipped;
on earth
could we ask for more assurance, that all will be well?
for surely, God has good plans for this blue planet;
and under the earth
could we wish for more certain hope, that evil is overcome?
for surely, the devil and all his works are destroyed.

No, on that day
we'll none of us have a leg to stand on
to justify the things we've done, or left undone

or a word to say
in our own, or others', defence

there we will all be on our knees,
the only words, worship.

Grape Juice

Isaiah 5:1-7; Psalm 80:7-15; Matthew 21:33-46

It would make a nice little retirement project,
I always used to think:
a modest vineyard in Tuscany,
sunshine, a little light pruning
and long evenings enjoying the fruits of our labours . . .

moonshine, more like:
castles in Spain (or Italy, rather),
daydream of one largely unaware
of the demands of husbandry
or the state of her bank balance.

Last year in Europe
helped to remedy that first gap in my education;
marvelling at the dedication
of those who strip every leaf that would shade the fruit,
and who strip the small fruit that would steal
from the main crop, on which rests
the owner's reputation for top quality wine,
mainly exported;
marvelling at the steep, hostile land,
narrow, giddy steps scratching chalky white lines
up and down between the vines;
think of those heavy baskets, hot sun, rough stones,
vertigo.
Marvelling then at the excellent wine
I can buy for under a fiver
at the corner shop:
maybe I'll settle for appreciation
of the fruit of someone else's labours.

Because it's labour intensive, this vineyard business.

I guess that Europe won't be in the running,
though, for many accolades
when it comes to God's vineyards.

So much good stock
planted over the centuries
(once the Middle East lost its monopoly)
and propagated all over the world,
producing new and exotic blends
of faith in far-off places, where work is welcome;
where workers willing and empowered
by the Spirit poured out;
where water once more becomes wine
and enemies, friends.

But look how that good stock
has now withered, victim of centuries
of neglect and abuse, smothered
by pseudo-science, bruised
by stones thrown, tended
and attended now mainly
by the weak, too misty-eyed
to man the watch towers, too old to bend
to clear the ground, too few
to see the fences mended.

And I fear the day
when the owner of the vineyard will return;
I fear what he will say
when he sees the state of the crop,
the distraction of the workers;
when he tastes the unappetising, watery wine.
Not that the workers will kill
the messengers, or the Son (not yet, in the West)
but they will send them away, politely, labelling them
counter-cultural, an irrelevance.

No one now strips off the leaves
that shade the fruit;
rips out the committees, the coffee mornings,
the continuation of customs well past
their sell-by date that absorb
moisture and light,
time, money, and energy destined
to grow the fruits of the Spirit,
and new fruit for the kingdom.

No one now strips off the small fruit
that would steal from the main crop;
the good ideas we fooled ourselves
were yours – but they were mine, ours,
enjoying their hour upon the stage –
but which will never amount to much
and have stolen your lead,
deflecting, misdirecting your people
away from your best: which have diluted,
divided and ruled.

And, Lord, I heard
they are using machines, blunt instruments
to pick the fruit, sucking in
good, bad and indifferent,
leaving lots of little stalks behind;
and I wonder, I do wonder
about Systems and Strategies,
Projects and Initiatives,
collective solutions
leaving lots of little individuals behind . . .

And, Lord, I'm not sure
I want you to come to my wine-tasting;
I'm no connoisseur, but sometimes I think
I wouldn't wish it on my worst enemy
and, to be honest,
I'd rather not drink it myself.
No way is it good enough

for the export market; in fact,
we're looking at bringing some over
from the second and third world.

Lord, you had hard things to say
to your top tenants, the Jews;
you trusted them with the best stock,
David's root and branch
but found only sour grapes.
And you will have hard things to say
to us, their successors
who have succeeded
in squeezing you out
only a little insipid grape juice

from vineyards which, frankly,
are a mess, a wilderness,
where weeds choke the vines,
poor soil and drought shrivel them
and blight goes unchecked.
The stock is still good,
still the best: but where,
oh where are the tenants
with the eyes to see
and the tears to weep,
the fire in their belly
and the will to work,
the cutting edge
and the strong back;

the refusal to settle for anything less
than the vineyards of Europe flowing again
with the wine of the Kingdom?

No Such Thing as a Free Lunch

Isaiah 25:1-9; Psalm 23; Matthew 22:1-14

I met him on the bend of a dusty mountain road,
struggling with a broken shoe,
and a pack that seemed too heavy for his years.
I greeted him, and he stopped, measuring me with his eye.
'Where are you going?' he asked.
'Wherever the road takes me.' I shrugged. 'And you?'
He smiled, and his face lit up.
'Me? I'm going home.'

'*Home?* But you surely don't live on a bare mountain,
where the clouds come down,
and wild animals howl and prowl?
Who would choose such a hard life, such a rough ride?'
'Choose?' For a moment he seemed nonplussed.
'It is chosen. And it is good: good to know
that I am going home, oh!
and such a home-coming!'

He set down his pack, and laid his hand on my arm.
'You could come too,' he said;
'such a feast! Plenty for all, and free!
You'd be welcomed, just like a long lost son;
come, do come! What do you say?'
'Me?' I was taken aback. 'Why would I want to come?
I don't even know where your 'home' is,
and I'm on my way . . .'

'On your way to – oh yes, wherever.' He met my gaze.
'Unpredictable
roads, weather and times,
don't you find? But to know that the dirt,

the exhaustion, the blisters, the rags, the scars
will all fall away, and a traveller like me is an honoured guest
when I finally reach home – that is,
where my father lives . . .'

'Thanks,' I said, 'but no thanks.'
I handed him back his pack,
surprisingly light,
and stooped to pick up my own.
'There's no such thing as a free lunch.'
He lifted his life's load onto his back,
and his eyes danced in his young-old face.
'Oh, but there is,' he said.

Many years passed before I met him again,
and he was not alone;
like the pied piper of Hamelin,
he had been joined by one, and another,
thinker, gaoler, rich man, poor man, terrorist, thief . . .
'Old friend!' He hailed me.
'Come, come and eat supper with us; come,
taste what is in store!'

There was something about his warmth,
his genuine pleasure at seeing me,
his generous spirit,
his simple joy in sharing bread;
but I wasn't sure that I was hungry, or,
as I looked at the company,
that it was the sort I wanted to keep;
or what it would cost.

'Thanks for the invitation,' I said
'but I really must be on my way;
places to go, things to do, people to see, you know?'
as I wondered uneasily where, and what, and who.
'Ah, yes,' he said sadly; 'wherever, whatever, whoever.
Are you sure you wouldn't prefer
to come home? My father's house
is famed for celebration:

music and singing to make your senses swim,
dancing that defies the pull of earth;
food of the angels,
wine galore at a word;
and clothes, new clothes to die for,
bespoke for you!'
'Thanks, but no thanks,' I said; 'I'm fine;
and there's no such thing as a free lunch.'

The last time I met him was in the winter;
those with him were more in number,
but not many more,
not many noble, or wealthy, or wise. And he said to me,
'Friend, where have you been,
and where are you going?
If you do not come home with me now,
it will be too late.

'There have been so many others along the way,
down the ages, who saw no need
to take note of the likes of me;
but their roads came to a dead end,
Jerusalem burned,
they were left without a Father, without a home,
with only the charred remains
of an unanswered invitation.'

I was tempted – just for a moment, tempted
to take the maverick seriously;
the thought of finding myself, in the end, at home . . . But no,
all that was surely away with the fairies.
I shuffled my broken shoe,
and shouldered my pack, too heavy now for my years:
and reassured myself,
there was no such thing as a free lunch.

Unholy Alliance?

Isaiah 45:1-7; Matthew 22:15-22

Well, it was never going to work, was it?
State religion, I mean.
The tying together of civic affairs and worship.

You can tell me how I must behave, if I am to live in your country,
but you cannot tell me what to believe, for I have a mind of my own.

So make your laws sensible, workable,
without the need for any threat of divine retribution
and leave me to worship at will;

make your laws consistent
with the common teachings of the great faiths
and spare my conscience;

make your laws few, but firm
and trust me, for my King's kingdom
is not of this world.

Was it you, Numa, first king of Rome, who started it all?
Bargaining with the gods, I mean.
Trying to get Jupiter on your side.

'I promise you sacrifices to die for,
if only you will power my armies
to sweep all before them . . .'

And so the knot was tied, the marriage prospered
until the kings grew slack
and the gods withdrew;

until Octavian, aware of the breach,
undertook the restoration:
eighty-two temples:

enough, to placate the gods?
But perhaps overstepped the mark, proposing
his own deification.

And I suppose Constantine thought
he was doing the Almighty a favour,
putting him in place of the Roman pantheon;

but with the wisdom
of several hundred years' hindsight
I'm not so sure
that the man who said
'Abolish religion!' unholy alliance of church and state,
hasn't got it right.

Religion is the tie that binds us
to the rule-book; faith is the leap of love
to catch the grace that sets us free.

Christianity is not a religion
  a philosophy
  a political ideology
  a moral imperative
  or to blame for the aberrations of all who have abused it;
it is rather the acceptance of a proposal from the Son of God
  to learn to love him
  to learn to live for him and,
  with all my fellow Christians,
  one day to be his bride.

You can tell me how I must keep the law, if I am to live in your country,
but you cannot tell me whom to love, for I have a heart of my own.

Even as I write,
they are protesting outside the House of Lords

that Caesar is claiming what belongs to God;
the state threatens to curb the state religion:
but what, if it will not bow?

For our God says,
'I am the Lord, and there is no other;
apart from me there is no God.'
There can be no arrangement, no accommodation:
we have no currency with which to bargain!
He will choose a Cyrus when it suits his purpose
but has no need to cultivate
media moguls, heads of state,
ethnic or religious minorities or majorities.
He IS
and we, bearing his image,
owe him our heart, soul, mind and strength

but if Caesar were to force a trial of strength,
what then?
Will the state disown its religion,
Christianity cut itself free
or God intervene?

Or, at a time when marriages
are made less and unmade
more and more,

will we, ironically, persist in cobbling this one together
which almost certainly was never
made in heaven?

For whose sake? For the sake of appearances,
or for the sake of the children?
Surely not:

Caesar is packing away his gods
like relics in the attic, finding them
uncomfortable bedfellows;

gods, and the godly, having
found themselves in a place of privilege
too comfortable

are losing their very godliness:
better, then, get out of bed,
shake hands

and, as good sparring partners,
sharpen one another,
iron on iron.

You could say, Jesus came
not to found a religion
but to abolish religion

(eat your heart out, all you atheists!)
and to replace it with the simple call
to follow him.

You can show me your teeth, and the length of the arm of your law
but do not try to make the sun rise, or imprison my soul.

Rooted

Leviticus 19:1-2, 15-18; Psalm 1; 1 Thessalonians 2:1-8

Sometimes, oh sometimes
I think it would be so good to be a *tree*:
no choices to make, just to *be*
and that would be OK:
rooted *here* and not *there*
an apple not a pear
accepting
the sap rising
leaves squeezed through
pink and white petals promising
particular fruit;
withering then,
wind-blown and bare,
waiting through winter
for spring . . .

And if someone were to say,
'This tree is in the wrong place,
it is getting in the way of my view,'
I would have to say, 'Here I stand!
I can do no other.'
And if they were to say
'I wish it were not an apple but a plum,'
I would have to say 'Come! I am what I am;
taste, only taste and enjoy.'
And if they complained
that my leaves were too green,
my complexion too pink and white
my fruit too well-loved by wasps
my winter-wear too austere –

well, I would have to say
'As the Lord wills: Amen and Amen!'

Blessed is the tree
that does not stray into other men's orchards
or bend over backwards to accommodate their views
or cross-pollinate with other fruit to suit their taste buds;
but its delight is in the Lord,
maker of heaven and earth
and apple trees.
It has no need to apologise
for his ways are perfect.
And he is like a man rooted in the love of God
who yields his fruit in season;
whatever he does prospers
(though it may not always look like it).

But I am afraid that my roots are shallow;
that when they say to me
'You are interfering with my view of the world;
there is no place here for such a stand,'
it is all too easy to bend, offer a few branches to the pruning shears;
when they wish I were less apple, more plum,
eager to please, I make myself up
and look too like apple for the connoisseurs of plums;
too like plum for the apple fraternity,
appealing only to lovers of novelty
who will quickly shelve me
when the new season's crop appears.

Why is it that my need for the approval
of my fellow men, that sucker that will never bear fruit,
seems so much deeper rooted than my need
for the approval of God?

I shy away from that call to be holy
because I am so anxious not to be labelled
holier than thou;
and I find myself in two minds about the approval of God

because I will not, I think, be able to bear
the disapproval of the crowd
   especially my neighbour
   especially my friend.

You ask me to love my neighbour
but I am not allowed to ask that he should love me;
you ask me to love my enemy
but there is no guarantee that he will thank me for it.
If I love you as I should,
then I will understand
that true love for others may be tough,
may not line up with the current wisdom,
the *Times* leader, the popular vote.
I will understand
that I must be prepared to stand alone,
stand, rooted by your river
even though the rest have upped sticks
and left in search of drier ground:
stand, trusting that in time
they may return
but if not, still I will stand
because I can do no other
and, shielded by your grace
from being blown about by every wind of doctrine, will bear
not resentment, frustration, regret
but, naturally,
fruit.

I used to have a poster which said
'Lives rooted in God are never uprooted'.

Lord, only when my roots go deep into you
will your love enable me to stand firm
to love those who do not love you
to love those who do not love me;
I must still ache for their love,
for I am human

but I will not be shaken
for that would be to betray them, myself, and my God . . .

    Make me, then, Lord,
    a blessed tree:
    rooted and grounded in you
    who are love.

Hook, Line and Sinker?

Revelations 7:9-17; Psalm 34:1-10; 1 John 3:1-3; Matthew 5:1-12

Saints
are those who have been hooked by the love of Christ
and who refuse to let themselves off the hook
when they realise what may happen to fish.

> Saints
> though, are still human. I am hooked, yes:
> but I wriggle and squirm on the hook, and sometimes ask
> to be put back in the water; next time, perhaps . . .

Saints
are those who have signed up for a new diet,
who commit to watching the weight of sin
and persevere through the pangs of hunger.

> Saints
> though, are still human. I have signed up for the diet, yes:
> but I tell myself I am not *too* fat, yet;
> I can afford to compromise: stave off those pangs . . .

Saints
are those who have entered the marathon
and who steadfastly turn up for circuit training
prepared to break through the pain barrier.

> Saints
> though, are still human. I have entered the marathon, yes:
> but as long as I finish, what does the time matter?
> Cut back on the training, ease the pain . . .

Saints
are called not to turn the world upside down
but to model a topsy-turvy living
which will challenge the world to take a different view.

   Saints,
   often in practice, though,
   have also got it upside down:
   we model ourselves on the world, and need
   ourselves to be challenged to take a different view.

Saints
are those who are poor in spirit: blessed
because we have come to the point
of knowing we can't cope;
we have been worn down, beaten down,
overwhelmed by so many obligations
we have come to the end of ourselves

and find that, unbeknown to us,
someone has opened a new account in our name
and all the resources we need
to bring in the kingdom of heaven
are ours.

   Saints
   though, are still human. We are comfortable
   with our own limitations, preferring to stay in control,
   set our own agenda, decide when enough's enough

   and so we sacrifice blessing for autonomy;
   and the world is not impressed
   by saints who have reached a sticking point
   and come to rest . . .

Saints
are those who mourn: blessed
because we have seen with the eyes of God
the tragedies of a world fallen from grace

and our own part in its downfall; we glimpse
what might have been, and weep
for a paradise lost

and find that God himself, Holy Spirit,
Comforter, is there; sharing not only the pain
but the certain hope, the promise that every tear
will be wiped away, and paradise regained.

    Saints
    though, are still human. We refuse to see
    how far we have fallen, preferring to mitigate blame,
    build castles in sand

    and so we sacrifice blessing for false peace;
    and the world is not impressed
    by saints who have reached a sticking point
    and come to rest . . .

Saints
are those who are pure in heart; blessed
because we will not indulge in lust or greed, but keep
our eye single, fixed on God;

Saints
are those who are merciful; blessed
because we refuse to judge, to condemn, to dismiss
but encourage redemption;

Saints
are those who make peace; blessed
because we do not insist, belittle or walk away
but work, with God, to reconcile.

    Saints
    though, are still human; we are soft
    on ourselves, hard on others,
    prefer the easy options

and so we sacrifice blessing for an easy life;
and the world is not impressed
by saints who have reached a sticking point
and come to rest . . .

Because we will not break through
our reluctance, although we are hooked,
but tell the fisherman 'So far but no further!'
we will not break through

because we will not break through
the pain barrier, will not, in the end
take God at his word, refuse the adventure,
we will not break through

because we will not break through
our fear that persecution will come
and that it's a threat, not a promise of blessing,
we will not break through

to impress a world
that is stuck in its own journey:
unhappy, unblessed
for lack of hook, line and sinker saints.

Prophet and Loss

Micah 3:5-12; Matthew 24:1-14

There they sit,
stereotypically
on the 7.10, studying *The Times*:
the literate
(my uncle could do the crossword
between Wimbledon and Waterloo)
the literate,
unable to read
the signs of the times.

They are an institution
and part of an institution
on which they rely,
in which they have invested:
the City, big business, the church,
the party, the law; imposing
structures, all pillars and porticos,
safe as houses,
safe as the Bank of England

just like the Temple
in the time of Jesus.

And the prophets preach
gilt-edged security,
off-shore tax havens,
spirituality (assorted),
political peace (where there is no peace)
and that humans have rights to everything:

false prophets.
Each has his price
and speaks with forked tongue.

In the short term, of course, it's much easier
to be a false prophet than a true one;
grow the beard,
buy the T-shirt,
find the agent,
do the photo-shoot,
plan the website
and always submit your copy to the editorial board
whose decision regarding punctuation,
sex appeal and political correctness
is final.

Just don't get it from God if you want to get a publisher.

Pardon?

Well, he's not much into punctuation,
sex appeal and political correctness.
More like war, civil and uncivil, famine, earthquake, persecution,
death, hatred, betrayal, deception, wickedness, disillusion . . .
Fine for the latest blockbuster movie or fantasy game
but to be told
this is *fact*
not fiction, and it's coming your way
hardly boosts the sales figures
or endears you to the messenger:

the true prophet.
Each pays a price
but counts everything loss for the joy of knowing Christ.

'Destroy this Temple!'
said the true prophet: and they did.
A hundred thousand captured,
ten times that number killed

when the Emperor Titus destroyed the Temple,
razed it to the ground;
forty years on, smoke rising for the last time:
sign that the times of the Jews had ended,
a new order had come.
'Not one stone left on another,' he said
and so it was.

Will we trust him, then?
Will we believe him when he speaks of another ending,
of the signs that the times of the Gentiles, too, are ending,
and a new order is coming?

And who will warn us?
Where are today's true prophets?
Who will dare to say
the diplomats are running out of patience,
the Banks out of credit?
McDonald's are running out of burgers,
and the Church out of truth?
Will God remain silent
because his prophets refuse to hear, or tell it the way it is?
Or do our prophets speak, hand their copy in
but editors overrule, ridicule, demonise?

Or is it that you and I prefer to shut our eyes, turn a deaf ear:
seeking assurance
from the grand façades of our great institutions;
each of us faithfully buying *The Times* on our way to work,
and failing to read the signs of the times,
failing to see our security's paper thin,
and the pillars and porticos are due to be dismantled
like so many sets on the world stage.

Will we believe Jesus,
our true prophet
when he warns us that things are going to get worse
before they get better?

Or will we cling to that frayed rope,
the illusion of utopia just round the corner
   when we've paid off our debts
   when democracy comes to the Middle East
   when renewable energy rules
   when the Imam shakes hands with the priest?

Forlorn hope.
It seems we are programmed
not to climb ladders
but to go round in circles
gaining ground here, losing it there –
and the prophets who cry 'Peace! Progress!'
who applaud our dizzy circuits
deceive themselves and us.

Where is the prophet
who counts it all joy, the loss of face,
loss of income or reputation?
Where is the prophet
who's filled with power, with the Holy Spirit,
with justice and might
to declare to our nation
that God is not mocked
and a storm of judgement is brewing?

Where is the prophet
who reads between the lines
of *The Times*
the signs of the times?

The Funeral of the Foolish Virgin

Matthew 25:1-13

The call had come at midnight.

The call always comes at midnight,
out of the blue, in the dark,
however long expected.

It caught them napping;
no time to make for the air-raid shelter
no time to mow the lawn or clean the car
no time to pay the arrears on the mortgage
no time to stock up on oil or excuses
no time to appeal, to apologise, to kiss and make up
no time to cover the nakedness
no time, even, to go to midnight mass.

And so I sit in her kitchen
at the table covered with notes on scraps of paper
as her mother fights back tears
and her father studies his hands
    as though he's never seen them before
and her brothers sit still like pieces of furniture
    wishing it would all go away
but the cards on the dresser betray the truth

and so I sit, and listen
to their story,
their cover story.

'She was a good girl . . .'

She was always a good girl,
even when the whole neighbourhood knew better

'She was a good girl,
she went to Sunday School, you know –
at least, she went on all the outings;
had a nice group of friends from up at the church,
used to do each other's hair and swap CDs;
she even went on one of these mission things;
she's still got the T shirt. Some of them were a bit serious, mind:
a bit straight-laced for her;
but she was one of them; she was *there*, you know...'

Yes, she was there; she, and how many others?
There – and not there.

I nod, and drink my tea
wondering, as always, how to focus fact from fiction.
'And later,' I say, trying to choose my words,
trying to lift the blanket of fog,
gently blow the cover story,
'did she have faith herself?'

But they cling like kids to the well-worn blanket:
they are C of E, the family has always been C of E
the babies have always been done,
and her brother sang in the choir;
me and her dad were married there, and her gran's
got a place reserved in the graveyard.
It's *our* church,
and she's one of us:
what more do you want?

What more do I want?
For a painful moment, I glimpse the divine lover
looking for a poem
and finding a tick-box form;
looking for someone on whom to lavish the world
and being presented with a Bill of Rights;
looking for a heart
and finding a solitary stone.

I hear the indignation,
I feel the confusion, the hurt;
and I know it is not their fault that they miss the point
when we have hidden it like a needle in an ecclesiastical haystack,
when we have offered the easy option
that doesn't work.
And I am indignant
and confused, and hurt
for them, and for her, and for God, and for all of us,
but I do not know what to do

and so I move on, feebly,
to ask about the service;
what music shall we have?
Her mother brightens: 'We've thought about that,
she was always her own person, you know;
knew what she wanted, did her own thing . . .'

I know what's coming; I can almost hear
the nail in the coffin

'We'll finish with 'I did it my way',
so much better than a dreary old hymn, don't you think?'
Perhaps she sees my face, misunderstands.
'No disrespect,' she adds;
'Maybe a hymn, too? We think there's one
about a shepherd? Something nice
and comforting.' Her voice shakes.
'It'll be so hard . . .
She was supposed to be going to that big wedding next week,
she was so looking forward to it.'

And I make notes
and sympathetic remarks
and organise the funeral
with sensitivity and skill

and curse my coward soul
that shrinks from telling the truth,
that God himself has died so that she can go to that wedding;

and I pray for my loveless heart
that cares less about their salvation, or my Lord's reputation,
than about taking the easy way out;

and I weep for my traitor church
that divides justice from mercy,
offering pious platitudes and false peace.

The call always comes at midnight;
if they are not ready, the foolish ones,
is it their fault, or mine?

The Reckoning

Zephaniah 1:7, 12-18; Psalm 90:1-8, (9-11), 12; 1 Thessalonians 5:1-11;
Matthew 25:14-30

I do wonder
whether I'll be there at my funeral
and, if so,
what I'll make of it all.

What will they say? How will they sum me up?
Will I be flattered? Furious? Frustrated?
Or perhaps no one will come
and I'll be gutted.

What will they write on my grave stone?
As the years go by,
will they mention my name
any more?

And will I regret
all that might have been
had I realised the adventure
of living and dying?

Maybe I'll look, from my place of *knowing*,
now, and be amazed
at how we underestimate
both life and death;

the investment, in me,
of such gifts and graces;
yes, and in you –
and the accountability;

or maybe I'll be too busy
coping with that final summing up
from the one who sees all,
knows all, weighs all

and I would ask for my time again
were it not for the fact
that hindsight
is no substitute for faith.

'Teach us
to number our days aright
that we may gain
a heart of wisdom'

and maybe
we should count backwards,
starting from the end:
from the day of reckoning

because although nowadays
we don't like to think of a God of judgement,
that's tough:
because he is who he is

and we can't say
we haven't been warned
or were unaware
of the ultimatum of death

or of his failure to inform us
of his estimated time of arrival,
thus giving us a chance
to revise

for the examination of our life's work,
to dig up our buried treasure
and spend it, spend ourselves,
with wisdom and hilarity.

I do wonder
if I'll be there, unable to protest
when they say, 'She always had time for us . . .'
Always? I don't think so

and often, with such bad grace;
when they say, 'She never spoke ill . . .'
Never? In your hearing, maybe;
and you can't hear thoughts.

For us, death seems to draw a veil
over all the imperfection;
perhaps we are thinking of what
will be said about us

and embrace an unusual charity;
and we pray a lot at funerals
for the mercy of God:
that, like us, he will turn a blind eye

(blind, ourselves,
to the faulty logic: that,
at any other time, we would look to him
for justice);

for the one dying,
though, often an unusual clarity,
a final honesty
before the facts

for, sure enough, in heaven
the veil is removed: nothing escapes
the divine recorder, and we will be called
to explain our workings.

'I entrusted you
with health and strength
and a father's heart:
what have you done with them?

'And you, I entrusted you
with a good brain
and a golden tongue:
what have you done with them?

'And you – you have had
wealth, and the skill
to gain more wealth:
what have you done with them?'

And I will have nowhere to hide,
no one else's answers
to crib or download:
for the first time

I will see how far short I fall –
and what might have been . . .
and I will be devastated:
as dust;

bowed by the enormity
of my complacency
and his grace: still
as in death

and then the stillness
seems to become a waiting;
I am not waiting, no: he is waiting for me
and I hear him say,

'And to all of you
I have offered forgiveness,
my gift of a new start, if only you dare
admit your need;

'to all of you
I have offered my Holy Spirit,
my very life in you, if only you also bear
the cross of self-forgetfulness.'

And I will see, *see*
what I glimpsed through a glass darkly:
the need that prompted me to cry out
'Jesus!'

And I will hear him say –
please God, I will hear him say –
'Death cannot hold this one:
she is mine.'

The Cat and the King

Ezekiel 34:11-16, 20-24; Matthew 25:31-46

Once upon a time, there lived a fat cat;
(there was, at that time, an obesity problem in the land).
One day there was a knock on the door of his executive-style home;
on the doorstep stood a thin man.
'Good day,' he said; 'I have something here that may interest you. May I
   come in?'
'Who are you?' said the fat cat. 'You speak well, but you look like a tramp.'
'I have fallen on hard times,' said the man; 'come down in the world,
you might say.'
'You may come into the kitchen,' said the fat cat, 'and tell me your story,
but make it snappy: we have drinks at seven, supper at eight;
I have a lot on my plate.'

The thin man sat at the table
sensing the quality, and the inequality.
'Well?' said the fat cat. 'What do you have that could possibly interest me?'
'I have the answer,' said the thin man.
'Oh yes,' the fat cat was becoming impatient, 'and what was the problem?'
'Your weight,' the other said calmly. 'You will not be able to get through
   the door.'
'Nonsense!' the cat laughed. 'The doors of my house are enormous.'
'This house, yes: for twenty, thirty, maybe forty years; but then?'
'But then, I shan't much care: by then, I'll be dead!'
'Exactly: what then?' the thin man said.

'Death's door, yes; that is wide enough
for all to pass through. But the doorway after that – to life?'
'Oh, I'll take my chance,' said the fat cat. 'I mean, who knows?
A bird in the hand, and all that: I've had a good life, done things my way,
creamed off some of the rewards,' he patted his stomach.
'We cats like to do our own thing; you know the old saying,

"Dogs have masters, cats have slaves"? Though I do try to treat people well.
No, I'll take my chance when the end comes.'
'No chance. And death is not the end, you know.'
The thin man stood and made as if to go.

'Goodbye – until we meet again.'
The fat cat shook his hand; held it an instant
'Nice talking to you. Er – would you like to take some bread and cheese,
a bottle of beer or two? For the road?'
The sun broke through the clouds and the thin man smiled.
'Thank you,' he said and, taking a battered notebook from his coat, wrote.
'I won't forget you.' The fat cat groaned. 'Now he's got me down as a
soft touch, he'll be back with all his friends.' He put the food in a bag,
    handed it.
'I'll come with you to the gates,' he said to his own surprise;
'I could do with the exercise.'

The thin man was back with winter
and, as the fat cat had suspected, a couple of mates.
'You look well, my friend,' he said. 'I think you have lost a little weight;
but one of your coats would still cover two of us!'
The cat was not impressed by the thin man's friends:
they were dirty, and spat, and would not meet your eye
but the thin man brought them into the kitchen, like he owned the place
and the fat cat turned out his wardrobe, turned away from the tears
of the friends as they fingered the fine cloth, which to him was the norm.
He joked 'I'll have to go jogging now to keep warm . . .'

And the strange friendship grew
and it seemed to the cat there was nothing, now
he could safely call his own; his comfortable life was disturbed,
was being, he felt, re-arranged . . .
To the thin man he complained one day 'My God!
What have you done? If it wasn't for you, I wouldn't, couldn't care less
about all these people: but since they are friends of yours – well,
I guess I must say, any friend of yours is a friend of mine;
but if I go on like this, I'll soon be as thin
as you!' 'Good,' said his friend with a grin.

It was late. The cat stretched, yawned.

'You mean I might one day be thin enough to get through that door of
   yours, if I keep up the good work, keep fit – that I might squeeze
   through?'

His thin friend shook his head. 'No chance.'

'All this counts for nothing, then? That I have lost, and others gained
   weight?'

'It counts as evidence: that you love me, trust me. And that is what counts.
The door that won't admit you on your own, on your own merit, is yet
wide enough for two.' He drew out his notebook. 'When first you let
   me in, I entered your name on the list of those *I will bring
home*, into my kingdom.'

'Your – kingdom?'
As he spoke, and the light outside faded,
the thin man seemed to burn with his own brightness.
'I am the poor,' he said
'but I am also heir to the riches of heaven.
Now I tramp the world: but the whole world will soon be under my feet.
I throw myself on your mercy: but I will be your judge.
I am the Shepherd, but I am also that door
of the sheepfold; only through me can you enter.
It is almost night. Are you ready?'